*The Idea
of a Christian University
in Today's World*

The Idea
of a Christian University
in Today's World

BEN C. FISHER

· MERCER ·

ISBN 0-86554-343-7

Library of Congress Cataloging-in-Publication Data
Fisher, Ben C.
    The idea of a christian university in today's world / Ben C. Fisher.
        xii + 164 pages   15 x 23 cm.   6 x 9"
    Bibliography: page 139
    ISBN 0-86554-343-7 (alk. paper)
        1. Church colleges—United States.   2. Christian education—
United States.   I. Title.
LC621.F57   1989   89-32828
377'.8'0973—dc30   CIP

320119

Contents

To
John and Mary Jane Dellenback
and
Norman and Millie Wiggins,
whose sacrifices and devotion
to Christian higher education
have inspired and made this book possible

Foreword

This book has been a long time aborning.

In the welter of work my husband did in his post as executive director–treasurer of the Education Commission of the Southern Baptist Convention, sometimes of a sunny Saturday morning we would sit on opposite sides of his desk in his office in Nashville, Tennessee, and take advantage of the unaccustomed quiet for him to compose a few pages on Christian higher education in general—removed from the everyday problems. He would dictate, and I took down in longhand what he said. Together we trimmed sentence structure, rearranged paragraph order, inserted transition phrases, and so forth.

By this same procedure, we often worked at the dining room table in Murfreesboro, North Carolina, after he retired; or at the desk in his part-time office at Campbell University; or in the study kindly provided by Chowan College; or in a hotel room or on seats side-by-side on a plane or in the front seat of our car if he had to make a trip to give a speech. I wrote what he said. We worked in the library of the Baptist seminary in Rüschlikon, Switzerland, in the Harvard and Boston University libraries, and wherever else we found the materials he needed to help crystallize his thought about the concept of a Christian university in today's world. He talked of it with scholarly friends in England and in Wales. He had it always in mind— clipping even the daily paper when it carried reference to the subject. His favorite bookshop had a standing order for works in related fields. Even in the last months of my husband's life, before he died in November 1985, he dictated to me from his hospital bed, and I have pages on which he laboriously printed out, on sleepless nights in the nursing home, sentences and outlines and references to be used in this book.

He knew, from his long service in Baptist higher education, from his discerning observation of Christian education in other denominations, from trenchant remarks of people in all walks of life who were his friends, and from his searches into institutions both in Europe and in the Orient, how badly Christian education is needed, how rare it is, and yet what a marvelous promise it holds. Therefore I have felt compelled to try to complete this book. Much of it had already been typed in third draft by the kindness of those at Campbell University; much of the expense had been taken care of by two grants from a donor through Campbell University and the Agape Foundation.

What Ben Fisher has to say about Christian higher education, therefore, comes from the wealth of his experience, the depth of his commitment, and the trust of others that he had something worthy to be said. I want his long labor not to be in vain.

Sally Fisher

Dr. Fisher's vision of the life of Southern Baptist educational institutions was a consummate one—one that we are pleased to honor with the publication of this volume. The Press acknowledges, however, that some of the books cited by Dr. Fisher necessarily represent knowledge that was available several years ago. There are a number of books that have been published within the last five years about Christian universities that simply were not known by Dr. Fisher in his lifetime. —ED.

Preface

For more than a hundred years, modern theology has been marching to an increasingly secular cadence. The traditional supernatural view of man* has been superseded by a completely rational outlook on his behavior and his place and activities in the world. As theology became more speculative, it tended paradoxically to affirm social responsibility on the one hand, but on the other to withdraw more and more from the actual human condition of suffering, strife, division, and hatred capable of the most bestial genocide. The Christ-centered gospel with its simple but uncompromising ethical demands was diluted until the very name of Christ itself, except in some oblique fashion, disappeared from the center of theological thought and writings.

The evangelicals followed just as certain a drumbeat to the secularization of the gospel, although it took a different form from that of the intellectual community. Evangelicals, with their simple pietistic propositions, came to rely on secular methodology for what had formerly been generated from the deep wellsprings of the spirit and tone of simple gospel preaching. Manipulated man was in many cases substituted for the regenerate heart and contrite spirit. Both the intellectuals and the evangelicals have now found themselves without the power of the revelation in Christ and his ethical teachings, which indeed could proclaim a gospel of an omnipotent God, fully and completely revealed in his son and in the Holy Spirit.

---

*Throughout this book, *man* and the masculine pronouns are occasionally used in the generic sense, meaning both *man* and *woman*.

One of the first tasks of the Christian university is to recover a Christ-centered gospel and to place once again revelation of God's mighty acts in history at the center of preaching and ministry. It is also important that the notion of the authority of the Scriptures be similarly desecularized. Recovery of the authority of the Scriptures does not require repudiation of scholarship, but it does require the reaffirmation of the primacy of revelation. The Bible is not merely a manifestation of divine logos; it is the Word of God—true, accurate, and all-sufficient for our self-understanding, the understanding of the world in which we live, and our salvation. In addition, with the deadening of spiritual values and the decentralization of the teachings of Jesus, it has become necessary for the Christian university to examine present-day crises in some detail.

This volume is dedicated to raising questions and defining issues that will help the Christian college to assert again the primacy of its role in reawakening and quickening the body of Christ: his church, his ministry, and his ultimate fulfillment.

CHAPTER 1

Seers and Prophets

Your old men shall dream dreams, your young men shall see visions.
—JOEL 2:28

Since World War II the term most frequently heard to describe higher education has been *crisis*. Who could doubt, in the face of overwhelming evidence, that these are days when higher education—whether it is public or private, Christian or secular, American, European, or Third World—is under judgment. The general verdict is that higher education in our time has neither a source of unity nor a clear-cut concept of values or purpose.

It is not as if, during this past half century, we had been without our seers and prophets, for many wise and good men have sounded alarms; but often they were not heard, and certainly they were not heeded. To put it another way, in our heyday of unlimited and unmerited optimism, we were in no mood for warnings. We did not stone these prophets; we forgot them. But their voices are being rediscovered, and we cite the following examples of those farseeing educators who spoke with eloquence and insight of what happens when sense of purpose dwindles, unifying principles disintegrate, and concrete goals are fragmented.

Sir Walter Moberly, in his book *The Crisis in the University* (1949) observed:

> The crisis in the university reflects the crisis in the world and its pervading sense of insecurity. Two world-wars have culminated in the threat

to civilization of the atom-bomb. The background of all that is planned or done in the years immediately ahead will be the imminent peril of world-wide disaster. We are living "in the midst of uncertainties and on the edge of an abyss."

This physical insecurity is matched by a moral and spiritual insecurity and indeed largely results from it. The menace to civilization consists, not in the discovery of atomic energy and the invention of the bomb, but in the presumed will to use it. It lies in the fact that the generation which has acquired these stupendous powers of destruction is full of fear and suspicion and that these notoriously govern the relation to each other of rival groups of the Great Powers. A state of war, says Hobbes truly, consists not only in actual fighting but in "the known disposition thereto." Coupled with this is the terrifying emergence of the underground man. To an extent which even fifteen years ago we should have thought incredible we have witnessed bestial cruelty, lust and lawlessness, not only as an occasional morbid aberration, but rampant and in power. The veneer of civilization has proved to be amazingly thin. Beneath it has been revealed, not only the ape and the tiger, but what is far worse—perverted and satanic man.

But the real trouble lies deeper still. It is true that the heart of man is deceitful and desperately wicked; to ascribe that view to the vain invention of "unpleasing priests" is much less plausible than it was. But our predicament is beyond cure by exhortations to individuals to a change of will and to "moral rearmament," needful as those may be. Our situation is due to the interaction of myriads of wills, each pursuing its own limited purposes, but for their accomplishment combining in larger and larger units, and finally producing a total state of things which no one foresaw and no one wanted, and in which the individual feels himself powerless because of the colossal scale of the influences which actually govern his life.

Moberly further states five critical categories of concern: dodging fundamental issues, engaging in false neutrality, encouraging fragmentation, accepting without criticism unexamined presupposition, and neglecting moral and spiritual values. [1]

---

[1] Sir Walter Moberly, *The Crisis in the University* (London: SCM Press, 1949) 15, 50-70.

In *The Crisis of Our Age* (1941), P. A. Sorokin saw the dilemma as a result of a rapidly developing sensate culture, in which all systems of truth and values follow the path of relativism. Sorokin almost half a century ago predicted what happens when a culture becomes preoccupied with sex and unrestrained pleasure.

> A quasi-pornographic conception of human culture acquires a wide vogue, in biographies, history, anthropology, sociology, and psychology. Anything spiritual, supersensory, or idealistic is ridiculed, being replaced by the most degrading and debasing interpretations. All this is closely analogous to the negative, warped, subsocial, and psychopathic propensities exhibited by the fine arts during the decadent phase of sensate culture.[2]

Just as serious a note was struck by the Committee on the Objectives of a General Education in a Free Society (1945). They saw the central problem of education in the United States as the loss of a unifying principle. While their report rejected Christianity, Western culture, response to change, and pragmatism as sources of unity, they were not very successful in defining what this unifying force is to be.

Perhaps the most often quoted paragraph of this report is its definition of the characteristics of an educated person: "General education, we repeat, must consciously aim at these abilities: at effective thinking, communication, the making of relevant judgments, and the discrimination of values."[3] The report's emphasis on values is particularly important, considering the scope of concern about values today. Of special significance to church-related higher education is the rejection of Christianity as a viable source of unity. However, the report does not preclude religion as a unifying principle for *church-related* colleges.

Robert Maynard Hutchins, in an essay entitled "The Education We Need" (1948), struck a deep note of pessimism, pointing out that one of

---

[2]Pitirim A. Sorokin, *The Crisis of Our Age* (New York: Dutton, 1941) 96.

[3]*General Education in a Free Society,* Report of the Harvard Committee (Cambridge MA: Harvard University Press, 1962) 73.

the tragic paradoxes in American education is that we may have reached a point where we have the power to annihilate—but not to rescue—the world.

> Where the American university cannot help us is where we need help most. Because of the paradoxes I have listed, because of our indifference to the real purposes of education and our preoccupation with the trivial, the frivolous and the immediately practical, the American university is gradually losing its power to save the world. It has the power to destroy it; it is ill-equipped to save it. What is honored in a country will be cultivated there; a means of cultivating it is the educational system. The American educational system mirrors the chaos of the modern world. While science and technology, which deal only with goods in the material order, are flourishing as never before, liberal education, philosophy, history and theology, through which we might learn to guide our lives, are undergoing a slow but remorseless decay.[4]

In the same period H. Richard Niebuhr, in his book *Christ and Culture* (1951), grappled with the enduring problem of the Christian witness in an ever-changing cultural context. Niebuhr's message is that the task of Christians is not to conform, but to transform.

> The time of the conflict is now; the time of Christ's victory is now. We are not dealing with human progress in culture, but with the divine conversion of the spirit of man from which all culture rises. "The kingdom of God begins within, but it is to make itself manifest without. It is to penetrate the feelings, habits, thoughts, words, acts, of him who is the subject of it. At last it is to penetrate our whole social existence." The kingdom of God is transformed culture, because it is first of all the conversion of the human spirit from faithlessness and self-service to the knowledge and service of God. This kingdom is real, for if God did not rule nothing would exist; and if He had not heard the prayer for the coming of the kingdom, the world of mankind would long ago have be-

---

[4]*Ferment in Education,* A Symposium at the Installation of George Dinsmore Stoddard as President of the University of Illinois (Urbana IL: University of Illinois Press, 1948) 37.

come a den of robbers. Every moment and period is an eschatological present, for in every moment men are dealing with God.[5]

Kenneth Irving Brown, in his book *Not Minds Alone* (1954), saw the necessity for facing up to the dual problem: secular society pronounces religion to be irrelevant, while at the same time the church-related college often seems apologetic for being related to the church. According to Brown,

> The irrelevance of religion is one of the predominating attitudes to be found during the first half of the twentieth century, when the structure of modern secular education, splendid in its strength, magnificent in its extensiveness, but nevertheless faulty and incomplete, was being refashioned.
>
> Even the church-related colleges came to be apologetic for their church connections and more than one sloughed off a relationship which had become an embarrassing tradition. The fetish of objectivity restrained many a conscientious instructor from making witness to his religious faith.[6]

A great Catholic educator, Jacques Maritain, pointed out in 1955 in his essay "On Some Typical Aspects of Christian Education" that, "if we wish to perceive what a Christian philosophy of education consists of, it is clear that the first thing to do is to try to bring out what the Christian idea of man is."[7] He goes on to indicate that, since Christianity sees human beings in all their contradictions—body and soul, good and evil, natural and supernatural—a Christian education can give wholeness and the dimension of lifelong discipline to what would otherwise be merely fragmented and temporary training.

---

[5]H. Richard Niebuhr, *Christ and Culture* (New York: Harper & Brothers, Publishers, 1951) 228-29.

[6]Kenneth Irving Brown, *Not Minds Alone: Some Frontiers of Christian Education* (New York: Harper & Brothers, Publishers, 1954) 9-10.

[7]In Edmund Fuller, ed., *The Christian Idea of Education* (New Haven CT: Yale University Press, 1957) 173.

William Grosvenor Pollard, a nuclear physicist, in his essay entitled "Dark Age and Renaissance in the Twentieth Century" (1955), raised the question whether this era is capable of building upon its Christian heritage.

> Our basic difficulty is that we live in an age when our whole civilization has in effect lost the capacity to respond to its Judaeo-Christian heritage. Just as the dark age of a millennium ago was a period when Western culture had lost its capacity to respond meaningfully to its Graeco-Roman heritage, so the nineteenth and twentieth centuries are essentially another dark age in which the capacity of response to our other cultural root has now been just as thoroughly lost. To me the recognition of the truth of this quite sweeping assertion seems fundamental to a really meaningful grappling with the Christian idea of education.[8]

Alexander Miller saw as a major challenge the recovery of direction and dynamic in higher education. In his book *Faith and Learning* (1960), he emphasized that "it was Puritan Protestantism which gave to the New England colleges and, by the same token, to American higher education the last coherent account of its own function; which was in effect to supply . . . a learned leadership to both church and state."[9]

Harry Blamires, in *The Christian Mind* (1963), saw the problem as a surrender to secularism.

> There is no longer a Christian mind.
> It is a commonplace that the mind of modern man has been secularized. For instance, it has been deprived of any orientation towards the supernatural. Tragic as this fact is, it would not be so desperately tragic had the Christian mind held out against the secular drift. But unfortunately the Christian mind has succumbed to the secular drift with a degree of weakness and nervelessness unmatched in Christian history. It is difficult to do justice in words to the complete loss of intellectual morale in the twentieth-century Church. One cannot characterize it without hav-

---

[8]In Fuller, ed., *Christian Idea*, 8.

[9]Alexander Miller, *Faith and Learning* (New York: Association Press, 1960) 22.

ing recourse to language which will sound hysterical and melodramatic.[10]

The late Samuel H. Miller, dean of Harvard Divinity School, in a lecture entitled "Rivets and Reality" (1962), saw the growing absence of integrity as a basic problem. According to Miller, integrity is the rivet without which both the person and the society in which this person lives fall apart.

There are two sides to this basic question; the public side—how do we hold the world together, and the private side—how do we keep the self together. I take it that education which is not concerned with such an issue is scarcely worthy of the name. It is in a broad and very serious sense the moral responsibility of education to be concerned precisely with the integrity of the individual and at one and the same time, quite inevitably, with the nature of reality by which the world is sustained in some degree of meaning and unity.[11]

Foundational to any serious study of church-related higher education must be the report of the Danforth Commission entitled *Church-Sponsored Higher Education in the United States,* issued in 1966. For purposes of this study two general conclusions of the report are significant: (1) in many cases the statement of college or university purpose lacks clarity; and (2) frequently the statement on religious commitment is weak or nonexistent.

According to the preliminary Danforth report, entitled *Eight Hundred Colleges Face the Future*:

In general we find that most church institutions lack firm and carefully considered policies in these respects. Institutions commonly seek some evidence of religious affiliation in prospective teachers, but too often nominal church membership is regarded as sufficient. What is lacking is the expectation that the faculty member will be an informed,

---

[10]Harry Blamires, *The Christian Mind* (London: SPCK, 1963) 3.

[11]In *The Mission of the Christian College in the Modern World,* Addresses and Reports of the Third Quadrennial Convocation of Christian Colleges, 17-21 June 1962, St. Olaf's College, Northfield MN (Washington, D.C.: Council of Protestant Colleges and Universities, 1962) 4-5.

thoughtful churchman, who can relate his subject to the Judeo-Christian tradition. Such persons are rare. This is one of the most basic problems of church institutions today.[12]

A final reference is a cogent observation by Earl J. McGrath, former United States commissioner of education, in his book *General Education and the Plight of Modern Man* (1976).

The original point of departure for curricular reconstruction today lies outside the academy. It consists of a review of man's major problems and the conditions of existence which all citizens will normally encounter regardless of their individual intellectual interests or their chosen career. In sum, to succeed today where it miscarried yesterday, the reshaping of general education must begin not with a consideration of subject matter but with human problems.[13]

The foregoing material is representative, but by no means exhaustive. The range of spokespersons concerned about education is wide: pastor and priest, teacher and administrator, philosopher and theologian, historian and sociologist, poet and journalist. Although differing widely in approaches, all demonstrate remarkable agreement on the ills of education, and particularly on the general loss of a sense of purpose.

Perhaps the problem has been stated too sweepingly, as if there is nowhere any possible source of unity. It is precisely in this field that the church-related college can make a claim to uniqueness through a reaffirmation of Christianity as a unifying principle of all knowledge. Although some church-related institutions exhibit indecisiveness, vacillation, and insecurity in regard to their relationship to the church, they should—by their very nature—be strong in the area of Christ-centered values and goals and less susceptible than any other educational institutions to the crisis in purpose.

---

[12]Manning M. Pattillo, Jr., and Donald M. Mackenzie, *Eight Hundred Colleges Face the Future,* Preliminary Report of the Danforth Commission on Church Colleges and Universities (St. Louis MO: Danforth Foundation, 1965) 27.

[13]Earl J. McGrath, *General Education and the Plight of Modern Man* (Indianapolis IN: Lilly Endowment, [1976]) 50.

Alfred North Whitehead, in his essay entitled "The Aims of Education" (first published in 1929), may offer a constructive idea toward a more positive approach. "Except at rare intervals of intellectual ferment, education in the past has been radically infected with inert ideas. . . . Every intellectual revolution which has ever stirred humanity into greatness has been a passionate protest against inert ideas."[14]

Such lifeless ideas are just as deadly for Christian thought as they are for secular philosophy. What is needed is active and dynamic application of Christian thinking in every area of life. The mission, then, of the Christian university in today's world is nothing less than to become a Christ-centered community of faith and learning and to cause its graduates to go out committed to this way of life.

OTHER REFERENCES

Bell, Daniel. *The Reforming of General Education.* New York: Columbia University Press, 1966.

Heilbroner, Robert L. *An Inquiry into the Human Prospect.* New York: Norton, 1975.

Hutchins, Robert Maynard. *Higher Learning in America.* New Haven: Yale University Press, 1936.

McGrath, Earl J. *Values, Liberal Education, and National Destiny.* Indianapolis IN: Lilly Endowment, 1975. Reprint, Nashville TN: Education Commission of the Southern Baptist Convention, 1978.

Ortega y Gasset, José. *Mission of the University.* Translated by Howard Lee Nostrand. Princeton NJ: Princeton University Press, 1944.

---

[14]Alfred North Whitehead, *The Aims of Education, and Other Essays* (New York: New American Library, Mentor, 1949) 13-14.

CHAPTER 2

The Problem of Purpose

> But the final claim of Christianity on men and on universities is not a thought.
> It is the reality of Jesus Christ—His revelation of the love of God and of
> immortal life.
>
> —HOWARD LOWRY

The period from 1960 to 1980 might be termed the era of reexamination and reappraisal of the church-related college in America. Self-studies were carried out by many of the smaller groups and by all the mainline denominations, both by the denominational boards of higher education and by the institutions themselves. Books, monographs, and research papers were produced in great numbers.

A significant aspect of these studies has been given too little attention. In most of the literature published there is a noticeable absence of theological presuppositions and biblical references. This is in contrast to earlier studies in which men like Outler, Lowry, Miller, Brown, Williams, and others did not hesitate to relate Christian higher education to Christian doctrine and scriptural authority.

Another aspect of these studies is that, because of this absence of theological and biblical presuppositions, inquiries into the relationship of church-related colleges to their denomination sometimes resulted in a public-relations endeavor without much substance. Another weakness is the almost total absence in these studies of any notice or comprehension of the radical changes already taking place in the social milieu: social reform, development of technology, environmental problems, and the impact of atomic power—all changes that affect educational theory and practice.

In several of the better studies, an excellent case was made for the private liberal arts college, while religion was treated almost as an addendum. In some extreme cases it seems that what has developed is a religionless church-related college instead of a Christ-centered community.

At the opening session of the second meeting of the National Congress on Church-Related Higher Education, in Washington, D.C. (1980), Father Theodore Hesburgh said, "The significant thing is that we are here." By we he meant twenty-three different denominations coming together in Christian unity. This was the glory of the national congress. The weakness of the congress was the unwillingness of the participants to state any strong biblical or theological convictions. This lack is also evident in much of the otherwise excellent literature that the congress produced. On the institutional level, one church-related college did a lengthy study, the purpose of which was to develop a program for renewal and balance. In the entire study religion was never mentioned, directly or indirectly.

On the other hand, there are exceptions: an institutional contribution is a book by Robert Sandin, *The Search for Excellence: The Christian College in an Age of Educational Competition;* and on the denominational level, a book by Richard W. Solberg and Merton P. Strommen, *How Church-Related Are Church-Related Colleges?* Other exceptions would be some of the statements issued by Catholic orders and educators and the *Reaffirmations* adopted by the Association of Southern Baptist Colleges and Schools at the National Colloquium in Williamsburg, Virginia, in 1976.

The fact that these stand out so noticeably points up sharply the growing tendency to begin restatements of purpose by merely concentrating on a careful rearrangement of time-honored and well-worn clichés. Moreover, it is also obvious that statements of purpose often become weak apologetics, trying to satisfy the church constituency, the accrediting agencies, and the faculties—and seeking to state the purpose in such an innocuous way as not to jeopardize the receiving of public monies. Some institutions not only declare themselves to be "nonsectarian" but eliminate all references to religion except those that might be permitted under federal guidelines.

In addition, the statement "the church is not a college and a college is not a church" is frequently stressed to the point that both the nature of the college and the nature of the church are reduced to shallow and almost meaningless entities.

I do not denigrate totally these attempts to rework a statement of purpose, a task that should be undertaken at appropriate intervals. However, in this era the first question to be answered is, What is meant by Christian community? The fact that this difficult question has never been fully answered is no excuse for not making this the beginning point for any serious study of the purpose of a Christian college.

One of the most obvious aspects of a community of Christian teachers and administrators is that, first of all, it is a Christ-centered fellowship composed of Christians, who are bound together not only by love of God but by love of learning and love of neighbor. For the academic Christian community this commitment finds its highest expression in academic competence and in personal concern for the welfare of the student.

Another characteristic of the Christian community is that it exists in a real world where people are always torn between good and evil, hope and despair, joy and sorrow, peace and strife, love and hate, faith and doubt, freedom and bondage, security and insecurity, the spiritual and the material. Secular philosophers such as Martin Heidegger suggest that man is "thrown here" and out of his own resources and courage must find an authentic existence. The Christian community, however, is one in which, through Jesus Christ and the work of the Holy Spirit, individuals are able to find an authentic existence as the marvelous gift of God. This gift enables them to cope with all exigencies and endure all hardships; it removes all cause for despair. By thus beginning with an examination of Christian community, one is able to derive a statement of purpose for the university that is dynamic rather than static and that measures results in terms of Christian living and Christian fellowship as well as in transmission of knowledge and professional skills in Christian surroundings.

The New Testament states nothing more clearly than that a Christian community is a witnessing community. By *witnessing community* is meant the practice of sharing Christ. A nonwitnessing Christian community is a contradiction. By facing up to this fact, one can deal with the straw man of "indoctrination." Jesus never forced his view upon any person, nor did he suggest that his disciples do so, but a major responsibility of every Christian college is to provide the sort of opportunity that Christ provided for nonbelievers to become Christians, and for believers to have an opportunity to grow in grace.

Student conduct, particularly since the revolution of the 1950s and 1960s, has been a matter of debate and concern. The great teachings of Jesus have no meaning apart from community. Because of the often-misplaced emphasis on individualism, even Christian colleges may have been unwitting contributors to permissiveness, unrestrained appetites, and moral anarchy. Jesus reaffirmed the Ten Commandments, but he did so in the context of community, and it should be noted that of the ten, seven cannot be stated without reference to family and neighbor. An individual outside of community context may keep the letter of the Ten Commandments but violate the whole spirit of the teachings of Jesus. A person may not lie, steal, or commit adultery; he or she may also never have experienced compassion, concern, or self-denial in the Christian sense. If on a church-related college campus one begins to develop guidelines for student conduct *based on what the teachings of Jesus require of the Christian community,* the deadening effect of legalism can be avoided. Following such guidelines for a fuller, richer Christian life could become a joyous experience. Ethics in this sense is where the action is and extends to every realm of university life. To be dilatory or timid about developing such guidelines is to miss the whole point of Christian ethics. The goal must be, not to tell the student what he or she must not do, but to state unequivocally what the expectations of the Christian community are for developing life that is worth living and in keeping with the will of God.

While general principles can be laid down and agreed upon, every college or university must early and often make a decision about the kind of institution it wishes to be. There exist in America today four broad categories of Christian colleges: those related closely to their sponsoring body; those who maintain a loose and nonbinding relationship with their sponsoring denomination; those who retain informal relationships with the sponsoring body but actually have become private institutions; and the growing group of nondenominational and interdenominational Christian colleges.[1]

In the case of a college or university closely related to its sponsoring churches, one begins with the assumption that it is theologically, philosophically, spiritually, and organizationally a unique part of its denominational witness. Upon this assumption, then, the purpose of the university must arise out of the community's understanding of its biblical and theological presuppositions.

Unless it is granted at the outset that God did something in Christ that his churches are peculiarly instituted to transmit, it is useless to formulate a statement of Christian purpose. The early church was a Christ-centered fellowship of baptized believers who not only shared a mutual love of God and neighbor but had a sense of purpose and mission. Within the fellowship, it was a sharing community and was responsive to the simple but basic human needs: to care for the widow and orphan, to clothe the naked, to feed the hungry, to care for the sick, to visit the prisons, and to comfort those in distress. The parable of the Good Samaritan (Luke 10:29-37) was a final and inclusive definition of brotherhood. Moreover, the overriding commitment of the fellowship was to share the "good news"—to evangelize, to bear witness, to exhort men and women to become obedient followers of Christ.

Furthermore, early in the life of the young church, believers thought that it was God's mandate that they travel beyond the borders of their own community, in territory more often hostile than friendly, risking their lives, enduring poverty, suffering ridicule, going to prison, and making any sacrifice that became necessary. Nowhere is this type of commitment better illustrated than in Pliny's letter to the emperor Trajan, asking what to do about Christians who would not worship the emperor. Pliny reported that so stubborn were these Christians that two little slave girls under torture would not deny their Lord.[2]

---

[1]Merrimon Cuninggim, "Categories of Church-Relatedness," in Robert Rue Parsonage, ed., *Church-Related Higher Education* (Valley Forge PA: Judson Press, 1978) 29-42, has analyzed the degrees of church-relatedness in more detail.

[2]Pliny, *Selected Letters,* Introduction and Notes by J. H. Westcott (Boston: Allyn & Bacon, 1926), Letter 109, lines 24–26.

Besides evangelism and missions, the third great biblical mandate is to teach. Growth in grace is to include not only the spiritual but also the intellectual. The Great Commission (Matt. 28:19-20) makes teaching a matter of primary concern. Paul extended the idea of teaching in his preaching and in his letters to the churches. The universality of the church's responsibility to teach finds nowhere a more clear-cut example than in Paul's sermon to the Athenians (Acts 17:22-32), followed later by his witness in Corinth (1 Cor. 2:1-5).

Athens, cultural center of the ancient world, was dedicated to Pallas Athena, goddess of wisdom, whose monument was the Parthenon. It was the home of Pericles, Sophocles, Aristotle, Euripides, and many other intellectuals, whose ideas helped to shape Western government, architecture, drama, poetry, astronomy, mathematics, and art. Moreover, Athens was a great university city where Socrates taught in the groves of Academe and where Plato recorded his *Dialogues*. It was a center full of religious symbols and temples, although the intellectual community itself had gradually ceased to take seriously either the gods or religion. It was a city of good manners but bad morals, where political corruption abounded.

The two dominant philosophies in Athens were Epicureanism and Stoicism (Acts 17:18). The Stoic Seneca said, "To feel pain or grief for the misfortune of others is a weakness unworthy of the sage; for nothing should cloud his serenity." Nevertheless, the Stoics did maintain that all men are brothers, that the welfare of the individual is subordinate to the welfare of the community, and that men should seek virtue. However, for the Stoic, the ultimate way out was suicide.

On the other hand, Epicurus, while he did not deny the existence of the gods, felt that they had no interest in the affairs of men. Epicurus taught that happiness is to be found by seeking virtue and avoiding vices. For him pleasures meant the enjoyment derived from intellectual stimulus and attainment. However, by Paul's day Epicureanism had degenerated into the gratification of sensuous appetites.

In Athens, Paul set the example of confronting the intellectual community with the Christian gospel. His experience at Corinth sometime later demonstrates the Christian community's responsibility to bear witness to every human condition.

In contrast to the intellectual and academic community of Athens, Corinth was a Roman, not a Greek, city. It was a metropolis dominated by commerce—a bawdy, boisterous port city, famous for its houses of prostitution. Half a million souls dwelt here, including Greeks, Romans, Jews, and barbarians. When Paul preached in Corinth as well as Athens, he demonstrated that the teaching imperative of the Christian church is to serve all of humankind, regardless of race or condition.

The early church was fully human. It was often fractious, disorganized, and inconsistent. "O foolish Galatians, who hath bewitched you?" exclaimed Paul (Gal. 3:1). There were theological divisions and moral inconsistencies, pharisaical self-satisfaction, as well as outright dishonesty and lack of integrity. There were also some who would have used the fellowship of the church to advance ambitious personal and political ends. But because the spirit of Christ and the Holy Spirit were dominant, the church, in spite of its faults, was able to change the course of Western culture. A large part of this change is due to the fact that the church built its universities and colleges and hospitals and orphanages as a way of demonstrating the love of God the Father for his children. In many ways these institutions became Christianity's most powerful instruments of evangelism, mission, and education.

The early Christian church was a community of hope in a decaying and disintegrating social order. Long before the advent of Christ, the Greek intellectual community had ceased to believe in God or immortality. Aeschylus in his *Eumenides* has Apollo say:

> But when the thirsty dust sucks up man's blood
> Once shed in death, he shall arise no more.[3]

While much of the hope of the early church was in the expectation of the early return of the Lord, the firm faith in a personal immortality was the ultimate answer to pessimism. It is to be noted that, although belief in the imminence of the Lord's return was strong, there was no retreat or withdrawal: Paul made his missionary journeys, Luke began to collect both documents and oral tradition in preparation for the New Testament, and

---

[3]Whitney Jennings Oates and Charles Theophilus Murphy, *Greek Literature in Translation* (New York: Longmans, Green, 1944) 230.

the various ministries of the church within the Christian community were pursued with vigor. The idea that there was a passive awaiting is not true, except in the case of a few. Indeed, the hope engendered by a belief in the resurrection of the Lord gave to life a new meaning and to work a new joy.

Thus the nature of Christian community shaped the early church. Similarly the nature of Christian community should govern the content of a statement of educational purpose for a Christian university in today's world. The ethical and moral obligations of all members of a Christian university family are never to be determined solely by current cultural and social sanctions but are derived from the Christian community's understanding of the way to apply to current circumstances the Word of God, the teachings of Christ, and the leading of the Holy Spirit.

Christian university policy should be forged by the demands of Christian community. Actually the Christian university should therefore be a freer institution than one that is bound by changing external standards. The secular university espouses academic freedom because of its commitment to the pursuit of truth and because of the requirements of the accrediting agency. The Christian university satisfies these same demands, but more important, it seeks God's approval. "The fear of the Lord is the beginning of wisdom" (Ps. 111:10).

The Christian university's obligation to produce competent and responsible citizens also arises out of the prior commitment of the Christian community to achieve a society in which, ideally, there will be no conflict: in which the whole group tries to free and assist individuals to become all that they are capable of becoming, while at the same time, individuals never seek to advance themselves either at the expense of others or at the expense of the community. In the spirit of Christ they are motivated not merely by the fear of personal loss or the hope of reward but by their desire to please God and serve their fellow human beings.

No two institutions, even within a particular denomination, will have the same statement of purpose, especially because of the great variation in educational objectives and, to a much lesser degree, in theological perspective. But with the foregoing thoughts providing a broad background, the following purpose statement of Campbell University might serve as a model statement for a Christian university in today's world:

Campbell University is a university of the liberal arts, sciences, and professions which is committed to helping students develop an integrated Christian personality characterized by a wholeness that includes: a method of critical judgment; an appreciation of the intellectual, cultural, and religious heritage; and a sensitive awareness of the world and society in which they live and work with persons.

Campbell University is a Baptist university affiliated with the Baptist State Convention of North Carolina. Both in and out of the classroom, the university endeavors to present Christian principles to students and to foster their application to daily life.

The purpose of Campbell University arises out of three basic theological and Biblical presuppositions: learning is appointed and conserved by God as essential to the fulfillment of human destiny; in Christ all things consist and find ultimate unity; and the Kingdom of God in this world is rooted and grounded in Christian community.

Therefore, the mission of Campbell University, as a community of Christian scholars, is to:

provide students with the option of a Christian world-view;

bring the word of God, mind of Christ, and power of the Spirit to bear in developing moral courage, social sensitivity, and ethical responsibility that will inspire a productive and faithful maturation as individuals and as citizens;

transfer from one generation to the next the vast body of knowledge and values accumulated over the ages;

encourage creativity, imagination and rigor in the use of intellectual skills;

affirm the university's commitment to the belief that truth is never one-dimensional but in wholeness is revelatory, subjective, and transcendent as well as empirical, objective, and rational, and that all truth finds its unity in the mind of Christ;

frame university teaching in the context of a liberal arts education seeking to free persons to live more abundantly and securely in an ever changing social order;

foster stewardship in nurturing the gifts of the mind and in developing aesthetic sensibilities;

equip students with superior vocational skills, productive insights, and professional integrity.

This university sees the human vocation as living by faith under grace, with no conflict between the life of faith and the life of inquiry.[4]

The ministry and message of Jesus is from God to persons in community. The Christian university in today's world must ever be aware of its confessional nature, exalting the lordship of Christ and willing to be numbered among followers who have experienced his redeeming grace. Without this commitment, statements of purpose have neither coherence nor applicability.

Moreover, the community of scholars in a Christian university, while drawing a major portion of its faculty from its own religious perspective, must be a community that is also open to other Christians. Christian unity does not demand doctrinal amalgamation. It does not call for the bland blending of theological presuppositions, nor does it permit the shallowness of compromised faith. God in his wisdom has created a pluralism in which his confessing disciples may work together in freedom and faithfulness to advance his kingdom.

---

[4]*Statement of Purpose,* Campbell University (Buies Creek NC: Campbell University, 1984).

CHAPTER 3

The Nature of God

Out of the depths have I cried unto thee, O Lord.

—PSALM 130:1

In defining the nature of the Christian university in today's world, the starting point must be the beliefs that the Christian community holds about the nature of God. For these times a critical question is, Does God really exist?

Existential philosophy has made this a tricky question, to such a degree that three persons can say, "Yes, I believe in the existence of God" but can have entirely different meanings. The one can believe that God is entity and person; another that God is being or essence; the third that God exists only in the human psyche—but all maintain that they believe in God. There is a vast difference, however, between the personal God of William Temple and Tillich's God as ground of all being.

Moreover, one is confronted with such new terms as *Christian atheism, realized eschatology,* and *religionless Christianity.* To add further difficulty, radical theologians have claimed that God is dead. It would be helpful if those who rejoice in calling up the shades of Nietzsche would quote his "God is dead" in its full context: he also said that it was the Christians who killed him—not pagan religions, gross materialism, secular philosophy, or scientific discoveries, but Christians!

The question for today is whether we are confronted by God as a real being or as an illusion. Historically Christians have tried to affirm the existence of God in three major ways. The first approach was rationally to prove his existence by deductive philosophical arguments, including the ontological (argument from being), the cosmological (argument for the first cause), the teleological (argument from design), the anthropological (argument from the nature of man), and Immanuel Kant's "moral imperative."

The second approach has been inductive. The very orderliness of the world and of nature suggests the reality of God as one who creates order. Much evidence of God is to be found also in the very existence of human personalities. The self, in spite of inherent capacity for evil, has demonstrated creative power and worth that transcends any material explanation. Courage, mercy, sacrifice, and love cry to be accounted for. Also there must be taken into account religious experience, in which individuals have an overpowering and transforming sense of a higher Being.

A third proof of the reality of God has been the faith affirmation of individuals who not only claim to have encountered personally the reality of God but have demonstrated faithfulness unto death. Many believe that the most powerful reason for belief in God is the radical change in the lives of individuals through conversion experiences.

All of these evidences—deductive, inductive, and existential—are components of natural theology, which is the belief that much truth can be learned about God independent of any prior belief about Christ or biblical revelation. The contribution of natural theology to Christian thought has been considerable. Early church scholars drew readily on Greek and Roman philosophers, including the works of Plato, Seneca, Plutarch, and Epictetus, particularly in relation to ethics and moral law. Christian scholars who made use of natural theology in exploring biblical doctrine include Clement of Alexander, Origen, Augustine, and Thomas Aquinas, and in later centuries, John Calvin, John Locke, and John Wesley.

But natural theology, though indicative, is not sufficient. Without reference to special revelation, it leaves us in the same predicament that Plato described in the allegory of the cave. Persons chained with their backs to the light and their faces toward the wall of the cave see only the shadows of people, animals, trees, and inanimate objects. The shadows they understand to be reality.[1] Without God's special revelation in Christ, man lives forever in the shades and shadows and in the long twilight. Religion without revelation in Christ guarantees that what man sees of God in nature, or in rational thought alone, resembles God (as the poet said) only as mist resembles rain.

Søren Kierkegaard came to hold that there is such a vast gulf between time and eternity that the abyss cannot be bridged by human thought. Salvation, according to Kierkegaard, is the supreme paradox. The eternal God becomes man in time and is crucified. This paradox calls forth the leap of faith, a passionate decision of will, and not an act of intellect.

Karl Barth has been the twentieth century's most powerful spokesperson for the concept that there can be no real knowledge about God apart from God's self-disclosure. Barth was extreme in rejecting natural theology and discounting reason (although many scholars hold that in his later writings he seemed to admit some validity in natural theology). He pulled back into sharp focus the idea that human knowledge, unaided by divine revelation, cannot give a complete picture of God. Barth has been a much-needed antidote for those who have overemphasized one's ability to know God unaided.

The problem now, of course, is what it has ever been: the dilemma of speaking about an infinite God in finite language. This has been a stumbling block for both philosophers and theologians and has resulted in the development of a complicated linguistic analysis. Such analysis is concerned in the main with myth, symbol, metaphor, parable, analogy, and literal meaning. There is much disagreement. While Tillich insists that all statements about God are symbolic, Hartshorne maintains that language about God, to be meaningful, must be literal.

In a brief summary such as this, one can touch only some of the major issues, always running the risk of oversimplifying. But having asserted the limits of rational proof of the existence of God, one turns to consider revelation. Although this whole subject is treated more fully in a discussion of the nature of knowledge, the premise is that rational beings can take

---

[1]Oates and Murphy, *Greek Literature in Translation*, 554 (a reference to book 7 of Plato's *Republic*).

comfort in the deductive, inductive, and existential support for belief in the reality of God but that men and women are more than rational beings. For a redemptive knowledge of God they are totally dependent upon God's self-disclosure through his son Jesus Christ, through the Holy Spirit, and through the Scriptures.

Theism is belief that God as person, as entity, as a conscious, loving being who is both Creator and Redeemer, enables men and women to account for their existence, the world in which they live, and their ultimate destiny. Moreover, a personal God is the God who is seen in Jesus Christ, who has revealed himself over and over again in the Scriptures, and who, although above the world, is always in the world—not merely a categorical, philosophical concept but a conscious, living, loving person who both hears and responds to the faintest and most unworthy cry for help.

Only theism, therefore, is both valid (in that it can meet rational tests) and adequate (in that it can give meaning and hope to human existence). There is one God, a personal entity, who transcends both his creatures and his creation, has revealed himself through his mighty acts in history, and will continue to do so. The Scriptures are a trustworthy record of God's innumerable manifestations to his people. The Bible is also the testament of God's promises, the basis for his covenant with his people. The Scriptures, moreover, are a record of man's sinful nature—his blindness, arrogance, and alienation from his Creator—and a powerful testimony to the desperate need for reconciliation.

The task of the Christian university in today's world is to determine its own belief about the nature of God, not merely as an intellectual exercise, but also as an experience that arises out of the depths and inner resources of the soul. On this belief, then, can be constructed the ideals and goals of the university.

OTHER REFERENCES

See also the following works, each of which appears in *Great Books of the Western World* (Chicago: Encyclopedia Britannica, 1952), hereafter cited as *Great Books*. Berkeley, George, *The Principles of Human Knowledge.*

Locke, John, *An Essay concerning Human Understanding.*

Montesquieu, Charles de, *The Spirit of Laws.*

Pascal, Blaise, *Pensées.*

Plotinus, *Third Ennead.*

Spinoza, Benedict de, *Ethics.*

CHAPTER 4

The Nature of Man

Dehumanization has penetrated into all phases of human creativity. In making himself God, man has unmanned himself.

—NICOLAS BERDYAEV

Modern man has many analysts and many spokespersons. Philosophers, theologians, psychologists, sociologists, poets, artists, and journalists all tell us who modern man is, what he will and will not do, and—in the vernacular of a well-known author—"what makes Sammy run."

In the world-famous Keukenhof gardens in Holland there stands the grotesque statue of a man. The sculptor has made this man from the debris of war; plainly discernible in the figure are parts of a plane, a tank, a machine gun, a radio, and miscellaneous parts of unidentifiable machinery. An essentially faceless death-head stares out from under a bullet-riddled, battle-scarred helmet. This statue speaks to the disunity, alienation, and dehumanization of modern man. It becomes a powerful symbol of misplaced power, of the carnage of war, of hate, death, and darkness. It speaks to Lidice, Buchenwald, and My Lai; above all, it speaks to the violence of its age.

Western man is increasingly represented as confused, purposeless, sensuous, hedonistic, religionless, without hope, and on the verge of despair. A good question is, When did modern man become modern? What is really meant by the term *modernity?* Is there any difference, as human beings—that is, in physique, psyche, personality, or thought process—between ancient and modern man: for example, between the great Greek philosophers such as Socrates, Plato, and Aristotle and a modern Barth, Tillich, or Niebuhr? What is the distinction between the citizens of ancient Rome *as persons* and the present-day citizens of Tokyo, Beijing, Calcutta, Moscow, Paris, and New York? Has there been any change in basic needs, desires, fears, and hopes? Has there been any fundamental development in human nature?

The truth is that, from this perspective, modern man may not be so modern after all. If man as a person has changed very little, then what has changed? If people still need food, clothing, shelter, community, and hope—if their emotional drives and reasoning processes are basically the same—then it may be essentially *in their self-understanding* that they are now different.

Both classical man and Renaissance man understood themselves as being under the sway and influence of the transcendent. There were marvelous mysteries, unseen presences, and demonic powers. Greek literature, particularly the tragedies, reflected fate (sometimes described as a wheel of fortune), to which man was bound and from which there was no escape. This is vividly illustrated in *Oedipus Rex.* In Greek mythology, Prometheus paid a terrible price for lighting the secular fires of knowledge and self-understanding. Toward the end of the Greek age, however, philosophy had become secularized, and as one of their poets said, "Greece is a land where faith is dead, and un-faith blossoms like a flower."

It is paradoxical that the rediscovery of pagan culture in the Middle Ages gave Christianity the intellectual power and force to become a dominating drive in Western culture. Christianity's dominance continued through the Renaissance and was not seriously questioned until well into the eighteenth and nineteenth centuries, when the supernatural generally began to be suspect. Intellectual leaders like Bacon and Newton, though, were men of faith, holding a deep belief in a personal God.

However, with the coming of the English Age of Enlightenment and French rationalism, Christian humanism began to erode. David Hume said, "Religion has lost all specificity and authority; it is no more than a dim, meaningless, unwelcome shadow on the face of reason."[1] As early as the latter part of the seventeenth century, the Royal Society at the time of its founding set a significant precedent when it ignored religion as a valid field of inquiry, although prominent clergymen were among the directors.

So-called secular humanism has largely replaced Christian humanism and radically differs from Christianity in its understanding of the nature of man and of the world in which man exists. Many scholars attribute the present malaise of Western culture to the erosion of its Christian base without any replacement of a unifying principle.

This erosion presents the Christian university with one of its greatest challenges. For example, the oft-repeated statement in our time (particularly by some theologians) that modern man will not accept the supernatural should not be taken at face value. Note the flourishing of cults and Satan worship; the worldwide charismatic movement, which has shaken both churches and theological faculties; the proliferation of electronic evangelism; the growth of religious groups on college and university campuses, particularly outside the established churches; the exploitation of the supernatural in some of the most perverted ways in movies, cartoons, television programing, and science fiction; and the emergence of militant and mystic Eastern religions such as Zen Buddhism. Even in Communist-dominated countries, protest against suppression of religion is showing greater and greater strength and regenerative vitality. Moreover, technology itself seems to be creating something close to the supernatural when a movie like *E.T.* sweeps the box offices in every city in the United States. Apocalyptic in every sense is the scene of a host of young people borne above the treetops on their bicycles by some unseen force in order to help them save the ugly little stranger in their midst. And some in the scientific community are backing away from former hard-line materialism as the only explanation for the nature of man.

The Greek man, the Roman man, and the Renaissance man (and woman) lived in a social order where they seemed to be always confronted with infinite possibilities. There were new lands to be discovered, new

---

[1]Quoted in Os Guinness, *The Dust of Death* (Downers Grove IL: InterVarsity Press, 1973) 7-8.

countries to be built, new ideals to be achieved. Both classic man and Renaissance man thought that Utopia was possible. Plato wrote his *Republic*, Sir Thomas More his *Utopia*. Modern man has produced such contrasting ideas as are found in Aldous Huxley's *Brave New World*, George Orwell's *1984*, C. S. Lewis's *That Hideous Strength*, and Anthony Burgess's *A Clockwork Orange*. This vivid contrast between hope and cynicism is further emphasized by what Arnold Toynbee has called "the failure of nerve."

Modern man faces on every hand the finiteness of his existence. In the natural world he has moved from a surplus of resources to a rapidly diminishing and unrenewable supply. The hope that science can artificially reproduce minerals and metals in sufficient quantities to meet the needs of the growing world population is very faint. Even the very water and air are endangered. Space and other universes, which once seemed to offer man such infinite opportunities, in the light of more sober reflection now seem more like a shroud from which there is no exit. To give one example: a person would have to live a million years and travel at the speed of light just to approach the outer limits of the known universe. There is a new eschatology in the natural order. With the final flame-out of the sun, the seas will turn to ice, vegetation will vanish, and no life as it is now known will survive. This is not an exaggerated or fanciful picture. David Jeffery, writing in the June 1983 *National Geographic*, said that the sun has about a ten-billion-year life span and now, "at 4.6 billion years old, is about halfway through this process [of decay]."[2] The fact that this remark is found in a popular and widely read magazine indicates wide reader interest and concern for endangered life that is shared not only by scientists but by the general public.

Moreover, with our current nuclear arms man may not have to wait for the final flame-out of the sun. He may well self-destruct, purposely or accidentally. Neither classic nor Renaissance man had to face this possibility. Psychologists say that in these days not just adults but little children have nightmares about nuclear holocaust.

----

[2]David Jeffery, "The Birth and Death of Stars," *National Geographic* 163:6 (June 1983): 717.

Our response to these threats has been to develop a new and awesome technology, but our self-perception has deteriorated almost in inverse proportion to technical progress. We are dwarfed and belittled by our own machines as much as we are by the possibility of cosmic catastrophe.

It is an open question whether technology will be man's servant or "salvation" or the master that will enslave or destroy. Fantastic predictions about controlling climate, establishing communities in outer space, and mining and farming under the seas must be taken seriously. Headlines in local daily papers express the intelligent concern of church leaders about perhaps the most frightening new experiments of all, in the field of genetic engineering. An article by Richard Wolkomir in *Smithsonian* calmly states that "scientists have already thawed embryos frozen for eight years and grown them into normal mice. They calculate that embryos could be revived after centuries in the deep freeze."[3] While biological engineering has possibilities for good, it has even greater possibilities for evil and for further reducing man to a mere mechanical entity. Although once he thought himself to be created in the image of God, he complains often now of feeling more nearly like a machine.

Indeed, the omission of the problem of evil (or sin) is the fatal flaw in modern man's self-understanding. Humankind is perpetually bound by the chains of pride, malice, and greed—shackles that only the redeeming love of God can break loose. An examination of any present-day psychologist's records would supply quantities of objective testimony to guilt and self-pity, emotions that scar the lives of countless people who do not consider sin an intellectually respectable concept. The error of Rousseau's idea of the innate perfectibility of the "noble savage" is nowhere more cogently contradicted than in the popular modern parable, William Golding's *Lord of the Flies*. Precisely from Christianity's ability to recognize this problem of evil and deal with it redemptively does it draw its great strength. No secular philosophy and no other religion has this resource.

People in earlier times had a faith in the transcendent that for the most part remained unshaken. They really believed that they had supernatural

---

[3]Richard Wolkomir, "Aristocratic Mice Are a Keystone of Genetic Study," *Smithsonian* 14:2 (May 1983): 112.

resources. Man lost the splendor of his being on the way into the twentieth century.

Darwin, Freud, and Marx were pivotal in the process by which men and women came to have a new self-understanding, as each in his way reduced man from his former high view of himself. Darwin viewed him not as a creature a little lower than the angels but merely as a high point in the development of mammals; Freud pictured him as a being at the mercy of his own drives, particularly sex; and Marx insisted that his hope lies in the manipulation of the economic order (dialectical materialism). Moreover, in a manner of speaking, Marx substituted for the kingdom of God the kingdom of man—a Communist realm replete with prophets, martyrs, Bible (the *Communist Manifesto*), and a compelling missionary zeal to convert the world both by the strength of a great idea and by force of arms.

The task of the Christian university in regard to the nature of man is thus at least threefold: (1) it must speak generally to the error of man's self-understanding apart from God's self-disclosure; (2) it must reinforce those who are within the Christian tradition against the subtleties and pressures of a growing secular culture; and (3) it must speak forcefully the truth in love to the vast number who are both spiritually and intellectually undisturbed and therefore uncommitted. A prime responsibility of a Christian university is to clarify its own thinking about the Christian view of man. In times past, because insufficient consideration has been given to the difficulty of the task, refuge has been taken in theological generalities and philosophical tautologies, which result in an anemic concept that offends no one. The task is made even more difficult because the university is a community of Christian scholars from varied backgrounds, of disparate ages, with differing degrees of commitment, and for the most part necessarily interested primarily in their own areas of competence. Nevertheless, there must be general agreement on basic theological presuppositions.

What, then, is the antidote for atheism and agnosticism? In a fellowship of Christian scholars the community of learning must be first and foremost a community of faith. While a Christian university in today's world would not consider developing a creedal statement or compelling members of the community to sign articles of faith, nevertheless there are broad Christian tenets and doctrines on which there should be general agreement:

not any legalistic compulsion of the individual, but a theological understanding that is essentially consistent and that leads to joyous and fruitful witness. Discussion of such a statement as the following might be a starting point for the development of such an understanding:

> Made by a purposeful God, man is a special order of creation.
> He is a sinner who cannot be saved through self-understanding, but can be saved only through God's self-disclosure in Jesus Christ. The eternal message of Christian redemption is that man is not alone, and that every life has infinite value, eternal purpose and meaning, and eternal existence.
> Both reason and revelation have validity, but reason alone, apart from God's self-disclosure, is incomplete as a basis for man's understanding of himself or the world in which he lives and labors.
> God created man as an intelligent, reasoning being, and for this reason free inquiry must not be limited, and the questing and adventurous spirit must not be discouraged.

When the Christian university in today's world can sincerely and joyously view the nature of man according to the above presuppositions, then the penetrating vision of Dr. Albert Outler can be realized.

> The cardinal insights of the Christian center around the three great deeds of God—miracles if you like—Creation, Redemption, Consummation. These, in their three-fold unity, constitute God's revelation, His self-disclosure to His human creatures. The central revelation of redemption in and through Jesus Christ illuminates both the beginning and the end—creation and consummation.[4]

OTHER REFERENCE

Berdyaev, Nicolas. *The Fate of Man in the Modern World.* Ann Arbor MI: University of Michigan Press, Ann Arbor Paperback, 1961.

---

[4]Albert C. Outler, "Theological Foundations for Christian Higher Education," *Christian Scholar* 37 (Autumn 1954): 206.

CHAPTER 5

The Nature of Truth

What is truth? said jesting Pilate, and would not stay for an answer.

—FRANCIS BACON

A Christian university in today's world must come to grips once again with what it considers to be the nature of truth, the way this truth is known, and how it is to be used. The understanding of Christian truth must be directly related to the understanding of the nature of God and God's revelation in Jesus Christ and in Scripture. Truth must also be understood in relation to human existence and purpose in the world.

Ultimate truth can best be known in the context of Christian community. All Christian truth is existential in that we are commanded by Jesus not only to know but to do the truth. This is also the Hebrew understanding. The prophet Micah sets forth vividly the fact that the greatest ideas and ideals, to have meaning, must be translated into living action: "And what doth the Lord require of thee, but to do justly and to love mercy and to walk humbly with thy God?" (Micah 6:8). Three strong, active verbs give dynamic power to what otherwise would be static ideas: *do* justice, *love* mercy, or kindness, and *walk* humbly.

In the Sermon on the Mount Jesus urges his followers not only to be meek and merciful but to hunger and thirst for righteousness and to act as peacemakers (Matt. 5:5-9). Paul likewise beseeches Christians to put on love, live in harmony, and have faith that can remove mountains (Col. 3:12-15; 1 Cor. 13).

Sometimes the word *veritas* appears on university seals and in college mottoes. The word *veritas* denotes primarily the truth that is determined by thought, imagination, analysis, the constructive process of experimental science, and the logical projections of metaphysics and philosophy. *Veritas* in this broad sense describes not only what Plato and Aristotle meant by truth but what is generally considered to be the empirical approach to knowledge. This also seems to be the concept of the present-day intellectual community.

In his essay "The Theological Basis for Christian Higher Education," Warren A. Quanbeck has pointed out that theologians have frequently been content to allow the empirical approach to knowledge to go unquestioned.

> In the history of Christian thought, the Greek epistemological tradition handed down from Plato and Aristotle has been only rarely challenged. The traditional understanding of this position assumes that truth is an intellectual concern, a quality of propositions. Truth is accessible to man, can be perceived by the intellect, and can be used by man to gain mastery over his environment. It is important to recognize that the Biblical tradition does not placidly accept these assumptions but challenges them strenuously. [1]

This challenge can best be understood by examining the New Testament meaning of truth. The Greek word for truth appearing many times in the New Testament is *alētheia,* which literally means "without a veil." It never means *veritas* in the above sense. The truth of which the New Testament speaks is unveiled mystery. The revelation of this truth is always God's initiative, through the Scriptures, the Christ-event in history, and the presence and work of the Holy Spirit. This is the truth about the Creator and his creation. This is the source of man's comfort, the ground for his hope, and the assurance of eternal life.

---

[1]In Harold H. Ditmanson, Howard V. Hong, and Warren A. Quanbeck, eds., *Christian Faith and the Liberal Arts* (Minneapolis: Augsburg Publishing House, 1960) 39.

A major task of the Christian university today is to reconcile—but not merely blend—these two concepts of truth. For example, a critical issue for the Christian university in today's world is the origin of man. Is man a conscious, purposeful creation of God or only a natural variation from other forms of animal life? Descartes held that only man has a dual nature. For Spinoza, the human mind is a part of the infinite intellect of God. However, with the publication of Darwin's *Descent of Man,* a concept of the origin of man was set forth, differing from the traditional Christian view in two ways: (1) man is a member of the animal kingdom, not differing from other mammals except in degree; (2) man developed by a process of natural variation in exactly the same manner as other new species of plants or animals.

Such a view poses a serious problem for those who view man as a special and purposeful creative act of God. While some aspects of Darwin's theory are now being challenged, for Christian thought the essential problem remains. An omniscient and omnipotent God certainly can use any method he chooses, and from a rational point of view, we are much richer for those scientists who have ventured to explore and unravel all the marvels and mysteries of the universe. The Christian must fall back on what is negotiable and what is nonnegotiable.

What must always be negotiable is method and mystery, as man slowly, painfully, and step by step—sometimes with great courage—dares to use the mind and imagination and will that God has given him. These characteristics indeed distinguish us. Locke in his "Essay on Human Understanding" has commented, "Brutes abstract not."

What is not negotiable is God's revelation: that man is not a chance happening or merely a natural variation but the very apex of God's creation. Thus the challenge to the Christian university is to try to reconcile the rational truth about creation with the revealed truth.

However, several insights should be stressed. The Judeo-Christian concept of truth, as reflected in the Bible, makes full use of intellect, logic, and experiment. Truth in the sense of *alētheia* is never illogical and never finds itself in conflict with new facts or insights gained by reason, but its frame of reference must include the transcendent. Moreover, the Greeks valued truth for truth's sake—and also because of its power to advance man. The Christian pursuit of truth, on the other hand, is in order to know and obey the will of God. But the will of God must be done in the community, not merely discovered and hoarded in solitude or used to advance selfish ends.

Thus a loving, all-wise Creator has given human beings not only the source of all truth—whether empirical or transcendent—but the dimension of unity. Only in the acceptance of this unifying truth can one understand man, his social order, and nature as God's creation.

CHAPTER 6

Liberal Arts

There is a knowledge which is desirable, though nothing come of it, as being of itself a treasure, and a sufficient remuneration of years of labor.
—JOHN HENRY CARDINAL NEWMAN

It has been held traditionally that liberal arts studies provide the context in which the Christian view of education can make its greatest impact and the implications of the Christian faith can be most fully expressed. Historically, liberal arts education, in addition to transmitting knowledge and skills, has formed the basis for developing moral and intellectual excellence; achieving responsible Christian citizenship; creating an attitude of tolerance and understanding; affirming the dignity and worth of the individual; defending civil, intellectual, and religious freedoms; transmitting value systems; and developing just laws. Liberal arts education is deeply rooted in history. Both the Greeks and the Romans made a distinction between education for moral and intellectual excellence and mere training for the practical and useful.

Matthew Arnold's "Culture and Anarchy" emphasizes that Hebraism and Hellenism have been the decisive factors in the development of Western culture. Since the Hellenic estimate of man seems to be emerging as a stronger formative force in this civilization, Arnold's analysis can be most useful. Again pointing out Aristotle's definition of education as *knowing and doing,* Arnold's exposition of the long conflict between the Hebraic and

Hellenic influences may be summed up as follows: the Greeks' primary concern was with knowledge, the Hebrews' with practice. For the Greek, the ultimate concern was right thinking; for the Hebrew, right conduct. The Greek found the meaning of life in intellectual virtues; the Hebrew, in moral and ethical living. Another great difference between the two cultures is that, for the Greek, man was the measure of all things; for the Hebrew, God was the measure, and it was God who dropped the plumbline of ethical and moral law into the midst of mankind (Amos 7:8). For the Greek (and for the Roman), detachment was the summum bonum; for the Hebrew, the divine imperative was involvement.

A proper question for the Christian university in today's world is, To what extent has man once more become the measure of all things, pursuing knowledge for knowledge's sake to the exclusion of praxis? *Doing* is understood here, not in the sense of technology, but in the sense of putting into practice the highest moral and ethical precepts that inspire man's conscience. From the beginning of Christian higher education, the interest of the church has been in knowledge for the sake of pleasing God and serving others.

Origen founded the famous School of Alexandria because he had come to believe that Christians have an obligation to witness to the intellectual community. Origen reaffirmed the value of humanism but denied its adequacy. By the time of Augustine, the church had begun to interest itself in the total task of education as one of the strongest ways to advance the Christian cause. The founding of the universities in the Middle Ages was based on the critical importance of liberal arts for the church. Churchmen believed that these studies freed man's highest powers—intellect and will—for their most fruitful development.

Reformation leaders, including Luther, Melanchthon, and Calvin, strongly identified the advancement of the church with liberal arts studies. The Counter-Reformation produced great Catholic educators such as Ignatius Loyola; and in the nineteenth century, Cardinal Newman's *The Idea of a University* is an argument that liberal arts is central to a Christian university. The liberal arts tradition was continued in the United States with the founding of Harvard, William and Mary, Princeton, Yale, and Brown universities, along with a large number of other church-related institutions.

Having sketched this brief history, one needs to make clear that any serious study of the idea of a Christian university in today's world must take into account at least the three following facts:

1. Liberal arts education originated independently of Christianity.

2. Liberal arts education, as it was originally known, has suffered critical erosion during the past half century.

3. The term *liberal arts* itself has lost much of its original meaning; considering the present state of affairs, the Christian university in today's world must give earnest and courageous evaluation, both to nomenclature and to the content of humane letters.

The rapid advance and increasing domination of secular humanism in American education should come as no surprise to those who are knowledgeable about the origin of liberal education. While it was used by the church, it did not come out of the church, and it frequently fostered attitudes that were at odds with the church. Liberal education has always been deeply rooted in secular aims and ideas and has generally been elitist. It has been unable to go beyond an amorphous humanism in explaining the meaning of human existence.

Both external and internal factors have contributed to the erosion of liberal arts in the last fifty years in America. The external pressures include the demands of a society that expects, particularly of the universities, more and more services that have nothing to do (except very tangentially) with teaching: for example, research in such widely representative fields as nuclear physics, medicine, agriculture, public health, industry, social science, national defense, environment, and others. Moreover, the growing desire to make at least two years of college education available to everyone and the need for many students to begin to make a living almost immediately afterward has resulted in placing the main emphasis on vocation rather than on liberal learning. Whatever might be said to the contrary, what now exists—at the very best—is a liberal-arts-oriented church-related college or university, offering preprofessional and professional training.

Another decisive factor among the external pressures on liberal education is the fact that professional educators in both public and private institutions are no longer in control. They are not only badly divided among themselves about what should constitute an education, but they find themselves being bypassed, particularly by the changes that technology has imposed. Many major businesses and industries not only are developing their own training programs but are already offering experimentally some liberal arts subjects that present strong competition to university courses. While the Ivy League institutions still enjoy enormous prestige, they no longer control educational trends as they once did and have long since failed to provide a viable model for the church-related college.

The internal factors that have contributed to the erosion of liberal arts include, first of all, the influence of the German university system, with its emphasis on research and specialization; the general adoption of the elective system; and, for a time, the near-elimination of basic requirements for graduation (although these conditions vary from one institution to another, and most universities have now gone back to a core curriculum). Moreover, the external pressure for increased vocational training has not been met with any serious attempt to balance this technical preparation with a liberal education. A far more subtle but more serious internal problem is that now many second-generation teachers, with little or no liberal arts background, are occupying the classrooms. These teachers are extremely limited in their ability or desire to show how their discipline is a part of the integrated whole.

Shouting the shibboleth of "liberal arts" will not solve the problems that have accrued over several generations. The term *liberal arts* itself, for many, now has little meaning, even within the fellowship of teachers. Furthermore, although the liberal arts view of education was once a unifying force, a glance at almost any recent commencement program will show that it has at present few adherents, for by far the largest number of degrees are now conferred in the fields of science, teacher education, and business administration.

The answer for the Christian university is not to abandon liberal arts but to redeem both the term and the content, as far as possible, of the old liberal arts curriculum, particularly those subjects that enhance both the rational process and the development of character. Scholars are already speaking of the postindustrial, post-Christian, postmodern world—in which higher education stands accused of having little sense of direction and offering limited leadership. The private sector, with daring, imagination, and experiment, might regain a decisive voice.

One of the accusations directed at higher education today is that it is unable to prepare its graduates adequately for the future because of the rate of change. For this very reason the value of liberal arts should be reexamined because the nature of this type of education is to major on principles and general truths that can then be flexibly applied to specific situations and could very well be the best way to prepare for a constantly changing future.

In his book *General Education and the Plight of Modern Man,* Earl J. McGrath says that the solution lies in the direction of educational institutions' resuming their primary function of not only disseminating knowledge but returning to those values that give meaning both to personal and to civic lives. "No additional amount of knowledge, however widely distributed among the people, will help lift us out of the present morass of conflicting goals and ambitions."[1]

For the Christian university in today's world there is a strong challenge to develop a curriculum that will meet both today's and tomorrow's needs and at the same time reaffirm the value of liberal learning. As someone has stated, mere knowledge without the humanizing values of liberal education will develop future generations of highly trained barbarians. The major task for the Christian university in relation to liberal arts may not be so much a reexamination of the curriculum or a restating of educational goals as a matter of inducing the faculties to reassess their own knowledge and preparation in the wide field of Western culture. The trend toward specialization has been so intense in recent years, along with an increased focus on practicality and "relevance" of the public school curriculum, that both the teacher and the class are likely to have very sketchy background for considering the broad questions that liberal arts studies raise. Moreover, both students and teachers are now largely members of the media-oriented generation. The average high school student spends many hours a week before the tube. As one emerging teenager put it, "TV is the plug-in drug, and I'm addicted!" Books go unread, and higher education in this country may

---

[1]McGrath, *General Education,* 182.

be in the paradoxical position of having the finest libraries money can buy—accessible but scarcely used by faculty or students.

One of the claims constantly made by the Christian college is that the mission of the institution is to develop the whole person and to produce a morally responsible and socially sensitive citizen. Another claim is that the small size of most of these colleges engenders dialogue between faculty and students. If indeed the church-related college is serious about helping the student to make responsible decisions and, according to the ideal of Aristotle, to know and do the good, every faculty member must have an understanding and an interest far wider than his or her own discipline. Furthermore, if faculty are committed Christians, they will feel bound to prepare themselves to answer the deeper questions when they come.

One of the burning issues in today's world may be used as an illustration of the way in which a knowledge of the liberal arts can assist faculty members in shedding light on contemporary problems that come up in the classroom or in their personal association with students. The whole question of justice and of how people are to be governed under law comes up unsolicited in discussions on many different topics. How is this question to be addressed? It was a major concern of Plato and Aristotle, of Roman philosophers, and of the great thinkers in every age. While these thinkers show wide disparity in their concept of the origin and application of laws, they are in solid agreement that a civilized society has never been able to develop without a high sense of obligation to law. Then it is entirely proper to raise the question, How may students make intelligent decisions about the way laws should be made and the authority law should have—in short, about the whole subject of justice and freedom—if they have never been exposed to the best that has been thought on the subject?

For example, would students have a predilection for anarchy and violence if they had read and understood either the *Crito* or Thoreau's *Civil Disobedience*? Both Socrates and Thoreau broke the law as a matter of conscience and nonviolent protest. However, because of their deep respect for law—and knowing that people must live in an orderly society—they did not protest the penalties for their lawbreaking or expect to be exempt. Socrates' friends put him under all kinds of pressure, and even his enemies hoped that he would flee, but he refused to escape and voluntarily paid the price for not obeying the law. His reply to Crito is classic.

Has a philosopher like you failed to discover that our country is more to
be valued and higher and holier far than mother or father or any ances-
tor, and more to be regarded in the eyes of the gods and of men of understanding? also to be soothed, and gently and reverently entreated when
angry, even more than a father, and either to be persuaded, or if not
persuaded, to be obeyed? And when we are punished by her, whether
with imprisonment or stripes, the punishment is to be endured in si-
lence; and if she leads us to wounds or death in battle, thither we follow
as is right; neither may any one yield or retreat or leave his rank, but
whether in battle or in a court of law, or in any other place, he must do
what his city and his country order him; *or he must change their view of
what is just.*[2]

Socrates' words are forceful enough in a course in Greek literature in
translation, but consider how much more forceful they might seem if they
should be read or recommended by a professor in teacher education, sociology, or computer programming, whose familiarity with them and respect for them would add weight and make them seem contemporary and
applicable. (However, a teacher's knowledge should be sufficient to point
out also that, although considered a model, Plato's *Republic* is a badly flawed
document that sanctions slavery and the elimination of the physically and
mentally unfit and, some have said, laid the groundwork for twentieth-
century fascism.)

Representative thinkers who have exercised a profound influence in
the development of political theory and government might include such
later figures as Thomas Aquinas, Machiavelli, Locke, Rousseau, and John
Stuart Mill. No faculty member, regardless of his particular discipline, can
be the best teacher unless he or she is familiar with the thought of such
influential writers.

Thomas Aquinas in his *Summa theologica* says that all power and authority come from God and that the right to make laws has been vested by
God in the people as a whole. Might never makes right, he maintains, and
just laws are made for the common good. Ultimate sanctions lie not in authority but in the justice of the law itself. Bad men obey the law out of fear

---

[2]Oates and Murphy, *Greek Literature in Translation,* 480, italics added.

of punishment, according to Aquinas, but good men obey the law out of a deep inward sense of what is right and what best serves God and neighbor.

For an entirely different concept, one could find no greater contrast than Machiavelli's book *The Prince,* in which he sets forth the idea that ethical judgments are irrelevant to political theory and government. When a nation makes offers of peace while its armies are secretly gathering on the neighboring nation's frontiers for an all-out assault (as Hitler's Germany behaved toward Czechoslovakia) or when a nation breaks treaties, deliberately lies, and practices deceit even toward its own people, it is putting into practice Machiavellian philosophy.

Moving from the Renaissance to the period of the Enlightenment, one can find no document more influential in the long history of the quest for freedom than John Locke's essay "Concerning Civil Government." Thomas Jefferson and other framers of the Declaration of Independence and the Constitution of the United States leaned heavily on Locke, not only for ideas but even for phraseology. According to Locke, all men are endowed with certain "unalienable rights," and "governments derive their just powers from the consent of the governed." Locke also declared that, when a government becomes oppressive, people have a right to rebel. It is important to note that, while Locke became the great champion of freedom *under the law* and of the inalienable right of individuals *to make and change these laws,* he was equally firm in his view that citizens are not free to engage in irresponsible individualism that would trample the rights of others.

Somewhat later, Rousseau held that every person is born with the innate right to be free and that this freedom is best realized in a republic constituted by law and governed by citizens. Rousseau's belief in the perfectibility of man is antithetical to the Christian view of man, but his writings do contain many valuable insights on the nature of law and government, particularly as set forth in *The Social Contract.* For example, he says of the civil state:

> The passage from the state of nature to the civil state produces a very remarkable change in man, by substituting justice for instinct in his conduct, and giving his actions the morality they had formerly lacked. Then only, when the voice of duty takes the place of physical impulses and right of appetite, does man, who so far had considered only himself,

find that he is forced to act on different principles, and to consult his reason before listening to his inclinations.[3]

For a final illustration of the kind of background needed for fruitful discussions with students on freedom and justice, John Stuart Mill's *Representative Government* bears careful examination. Mill's was one of the first and most powerful voices for universal suffrage. In his day this was a radical idea that received much opposition. It was Mill's contention that all citizens—regardless of race, creed, color, or wealth—should be full-fledged voters. It was also his firm belief that, under democratic government, men and women may most readily improve their character. Mill asserted that good laws can be judged by the "degree in which they promote the general mental advancement of the community, including under that phrase advancement in intellect, in virtue, and in practical activity and efficiency; and partly [by] the degree of perfection with which they organize the moral, intellectual, and active worth already existing, so as to operate with the greatest effect on public affairs."[4]

The above illustrations are representative and have not included such critical works on justice and freedom as those of St. Augustine, Montaigne, Hobbes, Montesquieu, and, in American thought, Daniel Webster, Jefferson, Adams, Thoreau, Lincoln, and others. To sum up, the liberal arts tradition, at least in theory, has had as its goal to transfer from one generation to the next the best that man has been able to think and do, so that individuals may be able to appropriate and use it for their personal advancement and for developing just laws by which an orderly society may be governed. To carry on this tradition, every teacher must be at home in the broad intellectual, artistic, philosophical, and religious achievements of man.

No issue is more important today than the decisions that this and succeeding generations will make concerning the way society is to be governed. The one certainty at this time is that, as natural resources dwindle, as the population increases, and as nations are pulled closer and closer together, the very

---

[3]Jean Jacques Rousseau, *The Social Contract*, vol. 38 of *Great Books*, 393.

[4]John Stuart Mill, *Representative Government*, vol. 43 of *Great Books*, 338.

survival of man may depend on our ability to preserve what we have learned about how people are best to be governed in order to have responsible freedom. This may well be the dialectic of the twenty-first century.

The discussion above on law and justice is only one illustration of the type of serious question that students often ask and to which they often get a superficial answer unless their teachers have a wide background in liberal arts and a genuine desire to help students to broaden and deepen their thinking. It would be unrealistic to suggest that every faculty member should have detailed and critical knowledge of all the vast body of liberal learning. On the other hand, it would be not only realistic but highly desirable that faculty members be familiar with representative works and that they remain interested and alert and willing to draw on the vast treasury of ideas to assist their students to develop the knowledge and moral character necessary to make them whole persons.

CHAPTER 7

Humanism

For Mercy has a human heart,
Pity, a human face,
And Love, the human form divine,
And Peace, the human dress.

—WILLIAM BLAKE

The Christian university in today's world needs to reevaluate humanism, which had its roots deep in Greek and Roman culture, existed to a far greater extent during the Middle Ages than is generally understood, flourished in Italy during the Renaissance, spread into other countries as the Renaissance spread, and became the matrix out of which the modern world was born. Humanism in one way or another has touched every aspect of human existence: religion, philosophy, art, literature, the sciences, architecture, and politics.

The term *humanism* has many definitions but is most generally thought of as that force, particularly in a given field of study, that focuses on the individual, viewing man as a free spirit with infinite possibilities and encouraging self-confidence and self-respect. Humanism revolts against any authority that suppresses the freedom of the person. Consequently, this movement did free people in Renaissance times from the despotism of dogma and from the narrow confines of medieval theology and scholasticism.

One of the greatest influences of humanism has been on the universities. In Italy, the universities of Bologna, Padua, and Salerno moved from conservative, theologically oriented institutions to become more liberal schools where the most popular professors were no longer the theologians but the humanists. German and Spanish scholars were attracted, and they carried back to their universities the new liberal movement; later the humanist viewpoint spread also to France, Holland, and England.

The study of Greek and Roman literature became an all-absorbing interest, and the gospel of the classics was substituted for the good news of the New Testament. Moreover, a new respect for scholarship developed. New schools were established, and the building of libraries and the collecting of manuscripts became a passion.

However, all was not sweetness and light. As the new mood carried man further away from religious faith, it also led people into all kinds of excesses and contradictions. The same societies that produced great thinkers, artists, architects, and writers such as Dante, Boccaccio, Petrarch, Michelangelo, Brunelleschi, Leonardo da Vinci, Erasmus, Grotius, Sir Thomas More, Dürer, Rabelais, Montaigne, Cervantes, Velasquez, and many other representative humanists were also characterized by unbelievable savagery, brutality, violence, and assassination. Corrupt politics was a way of life; justice was capricious; and voluptuous living of the most degenerate kind was practiced.

Furthermore, in spite of the noble and idealistic sentiments articulated by the classic writers about virtue, freedom, responsible citizenship, civil government, and morality, there was often a wide gulf between the stated ideals and individual and social practice. A rediscovery of the "humanities" did not necessarily produce humane qualities and concerns, although many of the seeds of freedom, justice, humaneness, social responsibility, and democratic government were sown during this period. Later these seeds were to bear much good fruit in representative and constitutional government, separation of church and state, freedom of universities to do research and to publish, protection by law of basic human rights, the beginning of the abolition of slavery, enfranchisement for women, and so forth.

A significant characteristic of humanism was that it generated a spirit that was creative rather than imitative. Humanism as it later developed in Germany, France, Holland, and England produced results that were in each case original and distinctive.

For the Christian tradition, it is important to note the turn that humanism and the Renaissance took in Germany, where the greatest influence was in theology. Humanism opened the eyes of scholarship to a new way of viewing the Bible. As someone has said, the new spirit in Italy emancipated human intelligence by emphasis upon the classics, and in Germany it emancipated the human conscience by emphasis upon the Bible. While the seeds of theological discontent had already been sown by Wycliffe and Hus, it was inevitable that there would be a clash between the old theology and the new spirit of liberalism that had been released. Reformation and Counter-Reformation ensued.

From this point on, the cleft between the church and culture began to be real and decisive. But the excessive conservatism and intellectual stagnation of the church, particularly in the Middle Ages, has been emphasized to the point of disregarding the contributions of Christianity to Western culture. Freedom of conscience, religious liberty, and social responsibility are not primarily products of a reawakened classical culture but are the result of the tremendous influence of the personal life and teachings of Jesus Christ. Plato's *Republic,* for all its idealism, is a document lacking in some of the most elementary humane qualities. The Greeks, in spite of their intellectual, cultural, and artistic achievements, were still barbaric in their warfare, inhumane in their exposure of unwanted children, and totally supportive of slavery; in politics they never rose above the vision of their own state or city. Among the Romans, freedom was reserved for Romans, as were education, leisure, and most of the other elements of a good life. Rome is well known for its comparative toleration, but it also gained a reputation for its cruelty, ruthless conquests, and exploitation of conquered people. One looks to the classics for many evidences of civilization and refinement, but not necessarily for humaneness.

Moreover, the claims of humanism (in the sense of intellectual rebirth alone) should be tempered by recognition of other forces that led to the development of modern man, such as commerce, the exploitation of natural resources, constant improvement of navigation and other means of transportation and communication, and discovery of new lands. For example, it is quite likely that the rapid development of optics was pushed forward not so much by Galileo and his discoveries of the heavens as by the grain mer-

chants of Venice, who erected the Campanile in order that grain specula-
tors, identifying from this vantage point through the telescope the ships
coming into port, might thus be able to make a safe bid on the cargoes.
The telescope also became an indispensable tool of warfare and of navigation and, when connected to a level, of architecture and engineering. Even
in those days, more than has been admitted, knowledge for the sake of
knowledge was often supplanted by knowledge for the sake of practical application to the human situation. The success of man's efforts to improve
material conditions and increase his comfort and well-being further increased his self-esteem and confidence in his own powers, so that the new
developing materialism had both a philosophical and a practical effect.

Consideration of the state of humanism in today's world is a critical
challenge for the church-related university. First, it is to be noted that the
most radical secular humanism continues to espouse some noble ideas, including the dignity and worth of the individual, the full range of civil liberties, universal education, an open and democratic society, world peace,
social justice, and environmental concerns. Yet, secular humanists have
made a radical break with religion and in their own way have become as
dogmatic and as rigidly assertive as the medieval church ever was. All
theistic notions of God are rejected; the promises of salvation and eternal
life are represented as illusory and harmful; moral values, for the secular
humanists, derive their source only from human experience and hence are
wholly relative and somewhat inconsequential; religion is to them powerless to solve the problems of human living; and they totally reject any idea
of revelation and the supernatural. Moreover, some secular humanists assert that theism, deism, and modernism have all failed and should be discarded. The humanist's "social passions" arise out of a conviction that all
that humankind can expect is whatever is achievable in the here and the
now.

The best such humanists have to say about religion is that it has
remained a constant in the search for abiding values, although the greatest values affirmed by the Christian faith they utterly reject. Although
claiming tolerance, the more radical of the secular humanists seek con-
sistently to belittle religion, denigrate the church, and ridicule all belief in the supernatural.

However, man's struggle to ascertain the truth about God, himself, and the world in which he lives is as old as civilization itself. The following are some of the major concepts indexed by the *Great Books of the Western World,* indicating that the same concerns have motivated the thinkers of every age:

Art	Family	Law	Religion
Being	Fate	Liberty	Science
Cause	God	Love	Soul
Citizenship	Good and Evil	Matter	Theology
Courage	History	Mind	Truth
Democracy	Immortality	Nature	Virtue
Duty	Justice	Philosophy	War and Peace
Education	Knowledge	Poetry	Wisdom

While the subject matter of man's deepest thought has not varied greatly from generation to generation, the lesson to be learned is that, in the epic struggle for justice, law, freedom, and wisdom, each generation— and to some extent, each individual—must be constantly vigilant and fight the battle for ultimate values in every era and in every individual life. Moreover, these ultimate values must become not mere ideals; they must find application. Many seekers after truth fall victim to a kind of intellectual self-hypnosis and become forever observers and analysts, never participants.

Secular humanists, depending as they do on human strength and wisdom alone, treat the struggle to find and implement values as a bootstrap operation; in so doing they isolate themselves in the universe, which they admit they can never fully understand, and encapsulate themselves in a life that has no meaning or reality beyond conscious existence. Whatever their claims may be to the contrary, their individualism develops a priority over all community, and their moral relativism makes it impossible to achieve the great ideals of justice and humanitarianism that they so vigorously espouse.

From the founding of Harvard University to a point well into the twentieth century, America was not inaccurately described as a deeply religious Christian society. The judgment of de Tocqueville in this respect was virtually unquestioned. Also unquestioned were the theological views of the Founding Fathers and those who wrote the Declaration of Independence and framed the Bill of Rights and the Constitution. These documents are rich in references to the Creator and Divine Providence. However, men such as Jefferson, Franklin, Payne, and others were deists, not theists. Jefferson made this oft-quoted statement about Christianity: "A system of morals is presented to us which, if filled up in the style and spirit of the rich fragments [Christ] left us, would be the most perfect and sublime that has ever been taught by man."[1] The key word is *man*. H. Richard Niebuhr in *Christ and Culture* has warned of the danger of reducing the transcendent Christ, the divine Son of God, to a mere cultural manifestation of the highest good possible to man.

Understanding that the humanism of the Founding Fathers was merely deistic and not theistic makes it easier to comprehend the rapid and dangerous growth of "civil religion" and the consequences of this development for the transmission of religious values in general education. In this sense, at least, this age is rightly called the post-Christian era. Yet, it would appear that not many Christian universities are coming to grips with this problem.

If the Christian university does not understand the historical development of humanism, it cannot comprehend the decline of religion as a vital and necessary force in man's development. The hiatus between the cosmic and the earthly, between the supernatural and the natural, between religion and science, is as old as Western culture. That remarkable Greek, Democritus, who predicted the atom as a basic structure of matter, rejected any notion of a Creator or a First Cause, or any idea of a Divine Providence working with an end in view. Moreover, according to Democritus, the soul perishes with the body. It is interesting that, in his television series *Cosmos,* Carl Sagan cited Democritus as one of the early philosophers to free men and women from the superstitions of religion.

The battle is clearly already joined on what appear to be two irreconcilable issues: on the one hand, the concept of the existence of God

---

[1]Niebuhr, *Christ and Culture,* 92.

and his creative and redemptive relation to man, and on the other hand, a massive materialism that seems at present to be prevailing. The Christian university can be a decisive factor, and nowhere has the assurance that human beings can overcome materialism been more forcefully presented than in H. Richard Niebuhr's *Christ and Culture.*

The greatest weakness of the humanist's view of man is the total confidence that, under the right conditions, man will respond to the high ideals of justice, peace, truth, and good will. The humanist has been almost wholly unwilling to confront the problem of evil, even in the face of twentieth-century savagery, unexcelled or unequaled by that in any other known civilization. At the present apex of human scientific achievement, the sword is still mightier than the plowshare, and the relative size of modern defense budgets would indicate that violence is still considered to be the ultimate solution.

Humanism—like liberal arts—can be filled with Christian content, and if it is to serve the Christian university, it must be consistent with the university's understanding of and commitment to Christ. The time has come when the Christian teacher must be willing to "put on the whole armor of God," to abandon the posture of anemic, disinterested neutrality on every thought, every issue, and every condition that affects the destiny of man. Education can "accept again the moral responsibility to decide and teach—not merely select and report. It can accept in brief the terrible responsibility of the teacher. For without the acceptance of that responsibility, teaching—teaching at least for life— is impossible."[2]

---

[2]Archibald MacLeish, "The Terrible Responsibility of the Teacher," in *Ferment in Education* (Urbana IL: University of Illinois Press, 1948) 48-49, quoted in Kenneth Irving Brown, *Not Minds Alone* (New York: Harper & Brothers, Publishers, 1954) 85.

CHAPTER 8

Citizenship

The chief duty of the university is to produce good citizens.

—JOHN STUART MILL

Responsible citizenship is a significant issue in today's world. Certainly when the history of this period is written, major achievements must be recognized in the field of civil rights and social responsibilities. However, along with these important advances have come excesses and an overemphasis on the rights and privileges of the individual as against the needs and the rights of community.

Moreover, this generation has witnessed a general breakdown in integrity and morality. Scarcely a week goes by without new announcements of scandal and malfeasance involving those holding high political office. Within recent years both the president and the vice president of the United States were forced to resign. Members of the House and the Senate have served jail terms for accepting bribes while in office. No major profession—including law, the ministry, medicine, and teaching—has escaped tarnish. College and professional athletics have been racked by major scandal. But even worse is the fact that the list of common scofflaws and cheats, as represented in the following examples, includes those who are affiliated with churches: parents using prearranged signals on the telephone from children in college in order not to pay long-distance rates; ministers relying on radar detectors to avoid being caught for breaking the speed laws; farmers burning tax-free tractor gas in their personal cars; tourists from all walks of life pilfering linens, silver, and china from motels; employers paying cash for labor in order to avoid taxes; businessmen picking up blank receipts at local restaurants for padding expense accounts; and even ministers and church leaders asking for false receipts on purchases abroad in order to avoid paying duty.

The vast majority of these people would be horrified at the thought of stealing money from the telephone company, a motel, or the government; but these seemingly harmless aberrations may be the best indicators of the extent to which personal integrity has eroded. Part of the rationalization for such conduct is that individuals feel pitted against the law and society and think they are entitled to use any sharp practice they can invent in order to get what they believe is rightfully theirs. Furthermore, violence has become almost a way of life, and vandalism is a national problem. Not even cemeteries and church sanctuaries have escaped. The aged and those living alone are always afraid. City streets are deserted at night.

Refusal by thousands of students to register for service in the armed forces is another strong indication of the growing absence of love for country and unwillingness to put defense of the nation above personal interests. Such attitudes are a direct result of the long neglect in the teaching of citizenship.

One of the noble ideas of humankind in its long struggle to advance has been that of responsible and productive citizenship. The battle for human freedom, dignity, and equal rights under the law started a long time ago. It is particularly helpful to remember that Plato in *The Laws* (book 10) argued that the whole structure of government and its conception of justice must depend upon a right belief in God and that in the universe God is the ultimate power. The Athenian Stranger, speaking to Cleinias, the Cretan, and Megillus, the Lacedaemonian, makes the following observation:

> No one who in obedience to the laws believed that there were Gods, ever intentionally did any unholy act, or uttered any unlawful word; but he who did must have supposed one of three things,—either that they did not exist,—which is the first possibility, or secondly, that, if they did,

they took no care of man, or thirdly, that they were easily appeased and turned aside from their purpose by sacrifices and prayers.[1]

Aristotle in his *Ethics* and Sophocles in his *Antigone* were also concerned with citizenship. In Roman history, this concern is articulated by Lucretius in *The Nature of Things*, Epictetus in *Discourses*, Marcus Aurelius in *Meditations*, Tacitus in *Annals*, and Virgil in *Aeneid*. Responsible citizenship weighed heavily in Plutarch's *Lives*.[2] In the Middle Ages, largely dominated by the Christian church, citizenship is one of the twin themes in Augustine's *City of God*. During the Renaissance, any number of representative men of thought are found absorbed in this theme, including Erasmus, Sir Thomas More, Shakespeare, Bacon, and Hobbes. One recalls easily such later works as Locke's "Concerning Civil Government," Spinoza's *Ethics*, Rousseau's *Social Contract*, Tolstoy's *War and Peace*, John Stuart Mill's *Representative Government*, Gibbon's *Decline and Fall of the Roman Empire*, Thomas Paine's *The Rights of Man*, Thoreau's *Civil Disobedience*, and Maritain's *The Rights of Man and Natural Law*.

These names serve as a reminder that nations have not yet arrived at the fullest expression of citizenship in many areas of human rights and participation and that some of the best ideas on citizenship, from Aristotle and Plato to contemporary times, have been badly flawed by the practice of slavery, by the almost complete absence of women's rights, by discrimination against those who do not own property, or particularly by invidious distinctions between classes, minorities of any sort, races, or age groups. Even Immanuel Kant contended that there were many in the community not entitled to the full privileges of citizenship. He consequently denied suffrage to "everyone who is compelled to maintain himself not according to his own industry, but as it is arranged by others." These restrictions excluded from basic rights apprentices to merchants and tradesmen, servants not in the employ of the state, minors, and all women.

<hr>

[1]Oates and Murphy, *Greek Literature in Translation*, 578.

[2]This and the following paragraphs are condensed from Ben C. Fisher's "Traveler without a Ticket," *1981-1982 Supplement to the CIC Independent* (October 1981).

Although in the ancient world the high ideals of citizenship included training for public life, discipline of passions and appetite, cultivation of mind, development of body, and respect for and obedience to the state, even unto death, still there was no constitution or bill of rights such as citizens now enjoy, specifying the privileges to which a citizen was entitled and protecting those privileges by the full weight of the state's authority. Thus the new concept of citizenship—embodied in a bill of rights guaranteeing freedom of speech, freedom of assembly, freedom of the press, freedom to engage in the exercise of religion, and immunity from unwarranted search and seizure—also protects citizens legally not only from individuals who would encroach upon their rights but also from invasion by government itself, a fact that needs to be emphasized again and again in this age.

There is always the distressing question whether the good citizen and the good person are identical in virtue and what happens when good laws are twisted and abused, even for ostensibly good motives. Both Aristotle and John Stuart Mill are right when they say that the good citizen is one who is equally capable of ruling and being ruled. For the good and humane citizen the voice of inner conscience must be obeyed. Thus for people like Socrates there were moral laws higher than those of the state, and he was willing to die rather than to disobey that inner voice. Likewise Marcus Aurelius could give unqualified allegiance to the political community only as it embraced the whole human family.

Responsible citizenship ought to be a major goal of any philosophy of education, for it would seem to be axiomatic that educated persons ought to be useful to society as well as to themselves. Any government that sets up an educational system that does *not* produce responsible citizens commits societal suicide.

The development of good citizens is necessary in a republic such as the United States, which, to be productive, must have three characteristics.

1. Leadership must be both intelligent and of unquestioned integrity.
2. The citizenry must be literate, informed, and morally responsible.

3. The general climate must be one in which there can be an interplay—even a clash—of divergent ideas; in other words, there must be freedoms of worship, speech, press, movement, and choice of vocation, as well as a reasonable economic security so that citizens have an opportunity to earn their daily bread.

Thus it is obvious that, in order to produce good citizens, it is necessary to teach values as well as knowledge and skills. In this day there has been not only an erosion of such instruction but sometimes, even in high places, a repudiation of it.

Perhaps the greatest single failure in general education has been the neglect of values. The fact that the whole topic is highly subjective and difficult does not relieve American general education, public or private, secondary or postsecondary, of the responsibility for developing in the students high moral principles as well as intellectual excellence. This has nothing to do with indoctrination. Concern for indoctrination has become more and more a smoke screen for the intellectually incompetent, the morally uncommitted, and the ethically indifferent.

Moreover, both the speed with which new knowledge now confronts the individual and the ever-increasing social change make it imperative for us to be able to make an intelligent moral response. Computers recall but cannot think. They record but cannot make decisions. They store up knowledge but cannot have concern or compassion. They can create only to the extent of prior programming.

A young teacher in a recent conversation spoke with great insight into the nature of the problem. The fact is, he said, that we have badly misread today's college students when we think they are not interested in values and particularly in the principles that we hold as teachers. The self-esteem of students goes up, he says, and they actually become teachable when they perceive that they are being treated as whole persons who are interested not only in job preparation but in the vital issues that make life worthwhile. What students really want, he feels, is the kind of development that will give them not just spotty, compartmentalized units of knowledge but a synthesis that will provide a satisfying view of life as a whole. Teachers need not have reached the end of their own development—indeed, they ought still to be growing themselves—but their students must recognize in them a grasp of fundamental issues and a compassionate desire to have students attain a similar integrity of their own.

Many, like this instructor, have increasingly strong feelings about teachers, in either the public or private college or university, who assume the stance that their sole responsibility is to transmit knowledge and that the student's development of life goals and conduct while in the university are matters of concern only to the student. Such an attitude on the part of teachers reflects intellectual impoverishment and an extremely low view of the worth and dignity of persons. If a college or university is serious about its philosophy of higher education as it relates to the production of good citizens, its concern will be reflected, not only in the curriculum and the budget, but in the kind of intelligent, competent, balanced communicator who is employed as a teacher.

Citizenship, of course, must be expanded to take on worldwide responsibility, but it is also true that people who do not love, and would not be willing to die for, their own country cannot fully love or respect their neighbors in other countries. The recovery of patriotism in the original high meaning of that word is essential. Demosthenes in the First Philippic, delivering an address to the Athenian citizens in a time of great national peril, said, "Do not speak to me of mercenaries. I will have none of your paper armies."[3] The First Philippic is a moral more than a military challenge, a clear call to integrity and responsible citizenship in all areas of the Athenian life.

Moreover, the call to citizenship today is a clear challenge to defend this country with lives, goods, and honor; to respect the flag and the liberty that it signifies; to respect those who wear the uniform and insignia of military service, and to remember the thousands who have died, many of whom lie at the bottom of the seas or in unmarked graves on the far-flung shores of this world; to understand the growing materialism and the forces that seek to destroy individual freedom and democratic government; and to remember the greatness and unselfishness of this country. What nation ever treated its defeated enemies with such consideration and generosity as the United States has treated Japan and Germany, helping them to make full

---

[3]Oates and Murphy, *Greek Literature in Translation*, 814.

recovery from the terrible wounds of World War II? Without instilling in students the old idea of "my country, right or wrong" or a new isolationism, it still should be possible for the teacher to impart to students a pride in, and love for, their country and a desire to serve it as citizens. The responsibilities of patriotism are an expression in the political arena of the need to put moral principles into action in community.

Furthermore, the Christian university in today's world should be a constant reminder that responsible citizenship, for the Christian, ever has a transcendent dimension. The great truth that Plato discovered about the relation between religion and law has its ultimate fulfillment in the teachings of Jesus, who put love of neighbor beyond love of self and who asked the penetrating question, "What do ye more than others?" (Matt. 5:47).

CHAPTER 9

The University and the Law

Law is order, and good law is good order.

—ARISTOTLE

Gibbon once observed that, if one really wants to know what a nation has achieved, one should examine its laws.[1] The Declaration of Independence, the Constitution, and the Bill of Rights have become models of expressing and applying principles of representative government. However, it is to be noted that the pathway to free and representative government has been a long and tortuous journey, for which many have paid with their lives and fortunes. To remember this is to understand in part the present global dilemma about law.

Students in any university, but particularly in a Christian institution, should be led into an inquiry as to the origin, nature, and purpose of law: who makes laws, by what standards of justice laws are to be evaluated, and how just laws are enacted and unjust laws changed. The problem is not merely to rearrange ancient rhetoric but to spare no effort to focus the light of both the ancient and the more recent past upon our present condition. The liberal arts tradition should be brought into full play, and authors such as Plato, Aristotle, Aquinas, Hobbes, Montesquieu, Rousseau, Locke,

---

[1] "The laws of a nation form the most instructive portion of its history," Edward Gibbon, *The Decline and Fall of the Roman Empire*, vol. 41 of *Great Books,* 71.

Kant, and Hegel reexamined in terms of the current situation. The focal point of teaching should be to give the student a fresh understanding of both freedom and responsibility.

THE SECULARIZATION OF LAW

The gradual but steady secularization of the concept of law has had a profound and negative influence on American society, on institutions of that society, on government itself, and on the citizenry. By secularization I mean the removal from law of reference to God or any transcendent reality and (more especially in the context of the Christian tradition) the rejection of a God who creates and redeems and who has established moral absolutes— truths that are always applicable as an ultimate standard. Without this absolute dimension, there can be no morals, nor can there be any constant values. When there are no standards beyond those that individuals set at a given time for themselves, they are left with only warring opinions and a nervous neutrality.

This definition does not condemn wholesale all that is secular, for the secular is part of life. Nor does this statement call for disregarding or condemning thinkers who take a different approach to reality; as Paul said, "I am debtor both to the Greeks and to the barbarians" (Rom. 1:14). However, there is a necessary distinction between secular and religious interpretations of life. In Christ, for the Christian, is the ultimate standard for inclusion and exclusion. The Christian college, therefore, must take into account so grave a development as secularization, by which it is being increasingly challenged. The Christian institution of higher education is the place where there can be Christ-centered, biblically oriented raising of ultimate questions by persons of faith and learning.

From ancient to modern times, men and women have found standards outside themselves on which they have based their concept of law. The Greek philosophers sought a constant for the development of law in what they believed was the unchanging phenomenon of divine law. Greek literature is filled with illustrations of belief in some transcendent being and principles of justice. Antigone answers King Creon when he asks whether she has dared to transgress his law: "Nor deemed I that thy decrees were of such force, that a mortal could override the unwritten and unfailing statutes of heaven.

For their life is not of today or yesterday, but from all time, and no man knows when they were first put forth. Not through dread of any human pride could I answer to the gods for breaking these."[2] Socrates likewise frequently refers to God and appeals to divine law; and Plato's Athenian Stranger stresses "the divine goods" to be sought by lawmakers: wisdom, temperance, justice, and courage.[3]

The Hebrews laid great stress on God-given law. The Book of Deuteronomy sets forth in great detail the divine laws and ordinances by which the people of Israel were to be governed. The fulfillment of God's promise to make Israel a chosen people rested upon the willingness of the people to obey all of God's law, but they were also to love God and thereby claim the richness and glory of his promises. "Hear, therefore, O Israel, and observe to do it; that it may be well with thee, and that ye may increase mightily, as the Lord God of thy fathers hath promised thee, in the land that floweth with milk and honey. Hear, O Israel: The Lord our God is one Lord: And thou shalt love the Lord thy God with all thine heart, and with all thy soul, and with all thy might" (Deut. 6:3-5). In his *Summa theologica* Thomas Aquinas identified three kinds of precepts to be found in the old Hebrew law: moral, judicial, and ceremonial.

Jesus set aside altogether as mere legalisms the ceremonial precepts such as washing one's hands before eating bread, and he modified in a radical way the old judicial precepts, but he reaffirmed and gave a new and broader meaning to the moral precepts. "But those things which proceed out of the mouth come forth from the heart; and they defile the man. For out of the heart proceed evil thoughts, murders, adulteries, fornications, thefts, false witness, blasphemies: These are the things which defile a man: but to eat with unwashen hands defileth not a man" (Matt. 15:18-20).

The Christian tradition that followed, therefore, emphasized men's and women's responsibility to God for following the spirit as well as the letter of moral law. Further explicated in the Epistle to the Romans, the great gift of the new law, with love as its supreme motivation—even love

---

[2]Oates and Murphy, *Greek Literature in Translation,* 283.

[3]Plato, *The Dialogues,* trans. Benjamin Jowett, vol. 7 of *Great Books,* 643.

of enemies—was to bring people a new kind of freedom, even from death (Rom. 8:2-4). Jesus, as he said himself, came not to destroy the law or the prophets, but to fulfill; not to create antagonism, but to reconcile; not to set aside the old law, but to give it a new and broader meaning in human experience. And the new law was not only for the children of Israel but for each person everywhere. By trusting and loving God, people were to rise above legalism so that their longing to do right and to know justice came not out of fear of punishment and the hope of reward but out of love of God, neighbor, and even enemy.

Religious thinkers such as Aquinas, Hobbes, and Locke recognized the validity of natural law—the right to life, food, and shelter, the right to be free, and so forth. These were held a priori to be a God-given part of human nature. The vast body of English law traditionally has been based on the tacit or declared premise that there is a God who controls and guides the destiny of humankind. Certainly at the time of the writing of the American Constitution there seemed to be an affirmation of the Judeo-Christian tradition. The God of theism was understood to be one sovereign Lord, maker of heaven and earth, active in history and in human affairs. God was back of nature, and therefore the author and giver of *natural* rights, but he gave also *positive* laws, such as the Ten Commandments, and held individuals to account for their deeds. Moreover, man is—according to this tradition—a fallen creature; because of his imperfect nature, without the help of God he can neither create just laws nor judge with equity.

While Jefferson, Adams, Payne, and Franklin were deists, and not theists, nevertheless the God mentioned in the American Constitution was understood by the people of that day to be the God of the prophets, and above all the God of Jesus, Peter, the Apostles, and Paul. Divine Providence was a reality; the will of God was to be sought and acted upon; the whole earth and all the peoples and places and things were held to be God's; the Ten Commandments and the Sermon on the Mount were the guidelines for individual conduct and human relationships; and the promise of eternal life through Jesus Christ was humankind's best hope. Jefferson, in whatever kind of God he believed personally, would surely have agreed with Justice Story that, at the time of the adoption of the Constitution, the general, if not the universal, sentiment in America was that Christianity ought to receive encouragement from the State, so far as it is not incompatible with the private rights of conscience and the freedom of religious worship. An attempt to level all religions, and to make it a matter of State policy to hold all in utter indifference, would have created universal disapprobation, if not universal indignation.[4]

Observers such as de Tocqueville and Crèvecoeur spoke of the formative influence that religion exerted, not only in American government, but in every area of early American social structure. In his book *The Life and Mind of America*, Harvard historian Perry Miller points out that, in the early period of American development, Christians saw God as working to redeem the whole culture, not just to save souls.

This is not to say that Christians always agreed about the nature of God or had a clear understanding of his will. Fearful and outrageous things were done in his name. At the same time that love was being preached as the essence of the revelation in Christ, hatred, fear, and desire for vengeance caused people to commit terrible crimes in the name of the Almighty. Yet, however inconsistent or disputatious Christ's followers might have been, God's existence was for them never in question. Human beings were seen clearly as created beings who had both an actual and a potential relationship to the Creator. They were perceived as inherently imperfect, but with the possibility for redemption by and reconciliation with the God who made them.

The fundamental moral laws were viewed not merely as a contract between individual persons but literally as commands of God, which were not optional but obligatory. There were varying views on law, justice, and freedom, just as the ancients had different concepts of these relationships, but there was no question of the divine origin and authority of law.

However, beginning about two centuries ago, reference to natural law assumed a new significance. Long before the ink was dry on Blackstone's *Commentaries* (1765-1769), in which the author assumed that God was the source of all laws, whether found in the Scriptures or in nature, Black-

---

[4]Cited in Isaac A. Cornelison, *Relation of Religion to Civil Government in the United States of America* (New York: DaCapo Press, 1970) 127.

stone's presuppositions had been challenged by a minority of strong-minded men, who became the forerunners of the secular view of law.

Thinkers such as Rousseau and Hume appealed to natural law, but with a difference. For these philosophers, the natural laws were derived directly from principles to be found in nature, *without reference to divinity.* This difference represents a radical break with the traditional Christian view of man and creation. God was no longer to be considered creator of the cosmos and of humankind, nor giver of law, civil or religious. Nevertheless, for a time even this conflict about the origin of law did not change a certain constancy that the concept of natural law retained: that is, that people had some gauge outside their own experience by which to make and apply just laws.

In addition to deism, which has already been mentioned as a force among the Founding Fathers, two other strong movements within the cultural context had a tremendous influence upon the development of American thought. One was unitarianism, ably expounded by William Ellery Channing, a belief that found expression in a humanistic personal religion, exalting a love for God and a love for fellow humans (who were regarded as inherently good), but rejecting the divinity of Christ. The other powerful trend was transcendentalism, a movement much more nebulous and difficult to define, but one that represented the New England intellectual community's break with the traditional Christian worldview. According to this concept, God is a Universal Spirit and oversoul of the universe, speaking in individuals and nature, and thus making revelation, biblical authority, or dogma unnecessary. Both of these movements diluted the concept of God as a lawgiver or even as a figure active in history.[5]

In the nineteenth century, under the pressure of the new humanism and the Darwinian theory of evolution, the historic roots of the Christian tradition of law were all but severed. Through the influence of the new humanism, human perfectibility was substituted for the concept of sinful human nature. Darwin's evolutionary theory had a devastating effect on the idea of God as Creator and became also a formative force in changing the concept of law, which began to be regarded no longer as a gift of God but

---

[5]Joshua Weinstein, *When Religion Comes to School* (Washington, D.C.: University Press of America, 1979) 8-11.

as an entity that has its origin in the social situation and simply evolves, much as an organism might evolve.

Hasty application of the theory of evolution was apparent in many other fields of thought. The incongruity, even cruelty, of such application in a field like economics is easy to detect. Herbert Agar, in *The Price of Union,* calls it "the perfect creed for soothing the consciences of millionaires" and quotes John D. Rockefeller, who said in a Sunday school address: "The growth of a large business is merely a survival of the fittest. . . . The American Beauty rose can be produced in the splendor and fragrance which bring cheer to its beholder only by sacrificing the early buds which grow up around it. This is not an evil tendency in business. It is merely the working out of a law of nature and a law of God."[6]

Similarly Andrew Carnegie in his *Autobiography* wrote of his conversion to Spencer and Darwinism: "Light came as in a flood and all was clear. Not only had I got rid of theology and the supernatural, but I had found the truth of evolution."[7] Carnegie discovered in this truth "my motto, my true source of comfort," because "all is well since all grows better." Later he wrote, "We cannot evade it; no substitutes for it have been found; and while the law may sometimes be hard for the individual, it is best for the race, because it insures the survival of the fittest in every department."[8]

Such oversimplifications in the application of evolutionary theory to economics are easy to recognize. Not so apparent, perhaps, but just as deceptive are the fallacies that come from assuming an evolutionary progress in law. Yet, it would seem almost self-evident that, when the ancient idealism of the Greeks is ignored, when the biblical and revelatory tradition is rejected, and when even any sanction of natural law has been repudiated, the perceived relationship between law and a goal of justice is inevitably at risk.

---

[6]Herbert Agar, *The Price of Union* (Boston: Houghton Mifflin, 1950) 552.

[7]Quoted in Amaury de Riencourt, *The Coming Caesars* (New York: Coward-McCann, 1957) 179.

[8]Agar, *Price of Union,* 552.

The concept that law achieves improvement as an evolving entity end-
lessly responding to "the will of the people," as organisms achieve survival
by adaptation, is an analogy not borne out by the facts. Response to the
will of the people can be calamitous. Sometimes it has been expressed in
cruel persecutions and in bloody executions. The bloodbath following the
French Revolution was carried out with meticulous legality. Before each
execution the warrants were carefully read and signed.

Hitler came to power through the will of the people, who conferred
upon him absolute rights, through which he committed crimes against humanity. The Third Reich proclaimed that the mass execution of Jews and
the destruction of the elderly and the mentally and physically handicapped
were both just and legal. The complete captivity of religion was justified
in the interest of the state. The question is often asked, How could such a
state of law emerge in a society where philosophers, theologians, artists,
writers, and musicians had long been in the forefront in the civilized world?

The answer in part has to be the loss of both divine and natural law
as a basis of justice, leaving society with no standard outside of its own experiences. Relativism results. Right becomes what the government says it
is, provided that the government has the power of enforcement. The old
debate between Socrates and Thrasimachus is revived: Does might make
right? If so, says Socrates, then justice becomes mere expediency and has
no force or application beyond the will of might. In a society where laws
are so conceived and applied, no act of the state, however heinous, is unjust
or illegal.

In a democracy, the majority rules, and the will of the people is ex-
tolled as a cardinal virtue. "Will of the people" can, however, become a
slogan behind which revolutionaries mask their raw grasp of power and by
which politicians justify whatever new laws or regulations they wish to
promulgate. The French in the time of their Revolution and the Germans
in Hitler's day did not foresee what would happen, but they did delegate
powers that made excesses possible. The will of the people, or, to express
it another way, "the consent of the governed," is indeed basic to a democratic society, but it is a complicated concept and even in ancient times
was recognized as one that must presuppose two conditions: (1) that what
the people will should be just; and (2) that the people should have sufficient

wisdom and moral courage not to be misled. Unless these conditions are met, expression of the will of the people can become a travesty.

Note that these conditions imply not relativism but a moral standard. When human beings have no shared concept of justice that an inner conscience compels them to respect, both freedom and responsibility suffer loss. When men and women are motivated only by an unrestrained pursuit of their own self-interest—when the will of the people, instead of deducing their laws from a fixed pattern of divine law, allows the social context to set its own standards without reference to God or any absolute values— even good laws made by responsible people have little meaning. Those who consent to be governed need to have a high view of virtue, justice, and the rights of others. "Power to the people" and "the rights of the individual" are dangerous catchphrases, particularly in an age when traditional and ethical norms have been weakened by being perceived as relative.

One of the paradoxes is that unremitting emphasis on the rights of an individual is beginning to erode, if not destroy, all human rights and dignity. Just as dangerous as the tyranny of the multitude or the tyranny of an unjust ruler is the tyranny of the individual. It is easier to deal with the visible despotic and unfeeling tyrant than to overthrow the despotism of a host of demanding individuals. What needs to be recovered is Locke's insight that the individual must possess the self-restraint and concern for others that permit him or her voluntarily to surrender some personal freedom in order that there might be achieved a community of just laws.

Each generation, indeed, must examine the law as it applies to current circumstances. Harvard law professor Lawrence Tribe, a widely influential constitutional lawyer, has said, "The Constitution is an intentionally incomplete, and often deliberately indeterminate, structure for the participatory evolution of political ideals and governmental practices."[9] But in the past, through a rational process, necessary changes in human laws were deduced from the changeless standard of divine law. The withering winds of civil religion have swept across the land, and John Dewey's dream of values without any supernatural dimension has turned into a nightmare of value

---

[9]Lawrence Tribe, *American Constitutional Law* (Mineola NY: Foundations, 1978) iii.

neutrality, with tragic consequences for American education from the kindergarten to the university.

The relativistic approach to law and the absence of absolutes have pushed us more and more in the direction of a new Pharisaism. The letter supersedes the spirit of the law; hence, without regard to the intent of the law, particular circumstances in a case are given high priority, and technicalities assume enormous importance, sometimes actually providing a way to circumvent the law. The criminal, even though he or she has committed a heinous crime, goes free on a technicality; one person pays taxes while another escapes through loopholes; a person can work for a lifetime to establish a business and achieve security, and can lose it all on a technicality about a deed. The injustice may be so obvious that it is not even disputed and yet may be dismissed by the judge with a casual, "Sorry. That is the law."

It is a chief function of the courts not only to adjudicate the letter of the law but also to apply it according to principles of fairness. In a secular society, the absence of any standard outside of law itself leaves the process vulnerable to error, and sometimes even vicious.

The famous jurist Oliver Wendell Holmes, Jr., noted in his book *The Common Law* that "the life of the law has not been logic: it has been experience."[10] On the surface, this statement seems to have nothing to do with religion; but Justice Holmes carried this declaration to a broader conclusion. Law, according to him, is not a gift of God, nor can it be extrapolated from nature; rather, it is intelligent experience in a constant process of fluctuation and change. Then divine law has no meaning, nor does any Scripture have authority. No point of reference is absolute, and law becomes, in the final analysis, what the courts say it is: ever changing, ever relative, with no standard for measurement.

When most lawyers held personally the Judeo-Christian view of God and man, there tended to be in every court case an underlying concern that the decision would be in keeping with divine law; the direction now, except when there is compelling reason to do otherwise, is to make decisions

---

[10]Oliver Wendell Holmes, Jr., *The Common Law* (Boston: Little, Brown, 1881; 39th printing, 1946) 1.

that will not violate past precedents, even though those precedents might be in need of reexamination.

Moreover, lawyers have attained enormous prestige in modern society. "A phenomenon of fundamental importance for both the social and intellectual history of America is the amazing rise, within three or four decades, of the legal profession from its chaotic condition of around 1790 to a position of political and intellectual domination."[11] Legal scholars have noted that lawyers have long since supplanted the clergy as the most influential persons in American society, in one way or another touching almost every facet of life. Therefore it is significant when the cultural secularization that is affecting all the professions (including government, the relatively new and powerful field of communication, and teaching at all levels) has also profoundly changed lawyers, so that many have a conspicuous absence of religious commitment. This statement is not to imply, of course, that even the majority of American lawyers have discarded religion as an ultimate source of justice, but it does indicate a gradual loss of individual moral responsibility.

What, then, are the channels through which attempts are currently made to cope with injustice?

DEALING WITH INJUSTICE

One option, of course, is civil disobedience. The question here is when and under what circumstances the individual is free in conscience to disobey those laws that he or she believes to be in conflict with either natural law or God's law. This question is as old as Socrates, and as young as Thoreau in the last century or Gandhi or Martin Luther King, Jr. in this century. Civil disobedience played an appalling role in American colleges and universities in the 1950s and 1960s, leading to near-anarchy as well as the destruction of millions of dollars' worth of public property.

Some of the great minds from Plato and Aristotle to Hobbes, Aquinas, and Locke have grappled with this issue. Hobbes says that there is absolutely no justification for breaking the law, for he believes that both

---

[11]Perry Miller, *The Life of the Mind in America* (New York: Harcourt, Brace & World, 1965) 109.

written and unwritten law have their authority from the will of the commonwealth, and for that reason, "whatsoever he [the sovereign] doth, it can be no injury to any of his subjects; nor ought he to be by any of them accused of injustice."[12]

Nevertheless, a just person is sometimes so compelled by the burden of conscience that he or she will oppose unjust laws both as an individual and by joining those of like mind. Individuals have proven time and time again a formative force, sometimes altering the course of history and human events. By their courage and conviction they have been willing to sacrifice life, security, peace, property, or reputation in order to gain redress for those laws or customs that they held to be inimical to human dignity and well-being. To this extent one is not merely theorizing but dealing with a problem with which every generation of human beings who live under law has had to struggle.

In his *Summa theologica* Aquinas earlier took a different position from that of Hobbes. While he does not specifically condone the breaking of the law, he does not completely condemn it either. Aquinas feels that the common good might best be served by some acceptance of unjust law rather than to risk and disrupt the orderly process of government, unless that law demands a demonstrable transgression of God's commandment. Thus it would seem, for example, that where there can be demonstrated the kind of injustice that really undermines God's law as well as the community, a person must both speak and act.

Locke is much more specific. He says that, under certain conditions, people can and should rebel against unjust laws, provided that they have sought redress by due process of law and as long as the action involves a majority of the people—and then only when life, liberty, security, or the pursuit of happiness is in demonstrable danger.

While there is considerable disagreement between Hobbes, Locke, and Aquinas on the matter of civil disobedience and the breaking of law, they alike caution against even a just rebellion against unjust laws when this can lead only to anarchy, thereby destroying not only what is bad but also what

---

[12]Thomas Hobbes, *Leviathan*, part 2, "Of Commonwealth," vol. 23 of *Great Books*, 102.

is good. The ultimate appeal always seems to be to redress, through reason and law.

The legal channels chosen by the American system of government for achieving justice are, of course, the legislative, executive, and judicial branches of government, whose responsibilities are, respectively, to frame, carry out, and interpret the law. A deliberate system of checks and balances was incorporated into the procedure from the beginning. While the distinction between these powers was never absolute, the current tendency has been for the judiciary to assume more and more power formerly exercised by the other two branches.

One recent development has been the rising importance of judicial review, which has been in effect since Congress passed the Judiciary Act of 1801. This law entrusted tremendous power to the Supreme Court by giving it the right to pass judgment on the constitutionality of any act of Congress, and also to pass judgment on the acts of state legislatures. The high court thereafter became potentially a powerful instrument for social reform.

On the positive side, it is to be remembered that, following the Civil Rights Act, the failure of the church and institutions of the church to support desegregation led to the breaking of the logjam by this very process of judicial review. Both the church and its Christian colleges must admit that, had it not been for their own stubborn intransigence, much of the civil rights legislation would not have been necessary. It does not speak well for Christian universities that for the most part they remained segregated until they were forced to comply with integration laws or run the risk of losing federal funds. And earlier, while it now seems unbelievable, the sad and embarrassing truth is that many of the most powerful pulpits in both the North and the South spoke out in support of slavery, thus alienating much of the American intellectual community—a hiatus that has broadened with the years. By the middle of the nineteenth century, the American intellectual avant-garde were saying, "To be free, men and women must discard the yoke of religion."

Christian universities must be courageous enough to face both their own shortcomings and those of their sponsoring denominations. The unwillingness and inability of the church and the institutions of the church to recognize and correct social injustice paved the way for the courts to take the initiative. After civil rights legislation was passed by Congress, when the House and the Senate could not or would not act, and when the majority of the churches were silent and indifferent, judicial review resulted in court orders that broke down the barriers of segregation and ended generations of injustice for many Americans.

However, the extent to which judicial review has given the courts, and particularly the Supreme Court, powers that they hitherto did not exercise will continue to be debated, as well as the effects of these powers on various segments of American society. Serious questions are now being raised as to whether some decisions emanating from the power of judicial review become in effect laws in themselves, which have no roots in the Constitution. A second criticism is that opportunity is afforded individual judges to be termed activists in a special cause, particularly as it relates to social problems. A third assertion is that the concentration of power in the Supreme Court risks bypassing the consent of the governed. While this latter statement may be a little extreme, there does seem to be evidence that representative government has suffered considerable erosion. Perhaps the most notable area in which concentration of power in the hands of the state has established new norms and fostered new attitudes is the relationship between church and state—a knotty and difficult problem.

SEPARATION OF CHURCH AND STATE

Recent decisions by the Supreme Court have so broadened the definition of religion, for example, that it has been reduced to whatever the individual human conscience says that it is. [13] Moreover, court judgments that have religious implications are often settled without reference to religion. This secular approach to interpretation and application of law can be illustrated by several Supreme Court decisions.

A ruling on the highly controversial right-to-abortion law was not based on any theological, biblical, or even moral grounds but upon the Su-

---

[13]*United States v. Kauten,* 133 F. 2d 703, 708 (2d Cir. 1943), and *United States v. Seeger,* 380 US 163 (1965); quoted in John W. Whitehead, *The Second American Revolution* (Elgin IL: Cook Publishing, 1982) 102-104, 106-108, 222.

preme Court's interpretation of human rights—specifically, the woman's right to privacy, which was considered to override any right to life claimed for the unborn child (not a person within the meaning of the Fourteenth Amendment, according to the Court). It is interesting to note that Justice Blackmun did put in a disclaimer mentioning the lack of agreement among theologians, medical doctors, and philosophers on when life begins, as a factor forcing the decision. [14]

The Supreme Court has upheld Sunday as a legal holiday, not because of any religious significance, but on the assumption that a day of rest is for the benefit of citizens.

At present, apparently the wording "In God We Trust" will be left on coins. The phrase "one nation under God" will also be allowed to stand in the pledge of allegiance, the Court's reasoning being that the word *God,* or the reference to divinity, according to Justice William Brennan, "may merely recognize the historical fact that our Nation was believed to have been founded 'under God.' Thus reciting the pledge of allegiance may be no more of a religious exercise than the reading aloud of Lincoln's Gettysburg Address, which contains an allusion to the same historical fact."[15]

Reference has already been made to the Supreme Court's ruling in relation to the Selective Service Act of 1940 in *United States v. Kauten.* While the act itself granted exemption only to those who believe in a Supreme Being, Kauten, though he refused to say whether he believed or disbelieved in God, won his case by asserting that, to him, refusing military service was an act of conscience. The decision was further undergirded by a 1965 Court ruling that upheld conscientious-objector status for three men but enlarged somewhat upon the reasoning behind *United States v. Kauten,* namely, in declaring that the definition of religion must be placed in a broader context. [16] (These decisions are also significant as a move of the Court

[14]*Roe v. Wade,* 410 US at 159; quoted in J. Whitehead, *Second American Revolution,* 124, 223.

[15]*School District of Abington Township, Pa. v. Schempp,* 374 US 203, 303-304 (1963); quoted in J. Whitehead, *Second American Revolution,* 109, 222.

[16]J. Whitehead, *Second American Revolution,* 102-104, 106-108, 222.

to "define religion," important in the controversy over separation of church and state.)

In these instances, the specific decision of the Court is not the issue. The issue is the extent to which religion is being excluded from consideration in contemporary Court cases. The overwhelming evidence is that, whether the decision involves either "the establishment of religion" or the "free exercise," the secular view prevails, even though many judges and justices have claimed neutrality. Under whatever rubric—whether it be sociological law, legal pragmatism, American legalism, legal positivism, or evolutionary law—the ultimate result is the same. Religion no longer has any great weight in decisions that materially affect the daily lives of all American citizens and does not enjoy the kind of freedom accorded, for example, to the press.

The thorny question of separation of church and state is clearly becoming more problematic, not less so. According to John Wilson, in *Religion in American Society: The Effective Presence,* "The Supreme Court considered the meaning of the First Amendment clause with respect to religion only six or seven times before 1940, but since then has reviewed it some forty times. In fact, between 1951 and 1957, eleven Church-State cases were heard; between 1958 and 1964 twenty-two were decided; and the period 1965 to 1970 witnessed thirty-four decisions, as did the period 1971 to 1974."[17] While from the beginning there has been considerable confusion in the interpretation and application of the First Amendment, it has been only within comparatively recent years that the Supreme Court has held more and more that religious rights prevail only if they do not violate compelling state or federal interests.

While the First Amendment declares that there shall be no state establishment of religion, no interference by the state in the internal affairs of a church, and equal protection of all religions by the state, the Court's current stance raises extremely critical questions for American culture: (1) Is the state curtailing the practice of religion in order to advance its own

---

[17]John Wilson, *Religion in American Society: The Effective Presence* (Englewood Cliffs NJ: Prentice-Hall, 1978) 193.

interests? and (2) Although the state has proclaimed its neutrality toward religious practice, is this neutrality in fact limiting the practice of religion? Unfortunately, many of the staunchest supporters of separation of church and state, who for the most part are members of the older established Protestant churches, have for the last quarter of a century addressed only the narrower issues, focusing major efforts on minor problems while greater dilemmas remain unsolved. Two such struggles have pitted Protestants against Catholics on federal aid to parochial schools and on government representation at the Vatican; another concerns prayer in public schools.

In fairness, however, it must be pointed out that courts do not initiate cases but are responsible for adjudication only. Moreover, if the Supreme Court has ordered a certain policy to be followed in one state, the decision is *applicable* in all states, but unless court action is requested, the judges do not take the initiative in applying the decision nationwide. The power of the judgment is in the precedent it sets.

Also there are certain subtleties in the decisions that are sometimes overlooked. For example, while it is technically true that prayer and Bible-reading in the public schools have not been ruled out entirely, actually both prayer and Bible-reading, to be legal, must be done in such a way that no religious influence will be exerted and no religious values taught.

Not only in the courts, however, but also in the executive and legislative branches of American government has the evolutionary concept of law, for good or evil, given fresh flexibility to the Constitution and paved the way for greatly increased power. Dallin H. Oaks, former Utah Supreme Court justice and, prior to that, president of Brigham Young University, in his book *Trust Doctrines in Church Controversies* has pointed out the inherent dangers of expanding government regulation. Oaks sees an increasing intrusion of government into private activities.[18]

Congress and the executive branch have participated in the encroachment on rights formerly thought to be guaranteed under the Constitution to the church and institutions of the church. There has been a proliferation

---

[18]Dallin H. Oaks, *Trust Doctrines in Church Controversies* (Macon GA: Mercer University Press, 1984).

of the vast body of regulations promulgated by various government agencies. Congress passes general laws (too often in vague terms) that are then turned over, theoretically, to the executive branch for enforcement. The executive branch leaves up to the various government agencies the powers of both definition and enforcement.[19] Many legal scholars are pointing out that a powerful and persistent bureaucracy now constitutes, in effect, a fourth branch of government.

As a consequence, there has developed a growing adversary relationship between the government and educational institutions, public and private. Church-related colleges are peculiarly affected. Constant litigation, expensive and time-consuming, is in process as institutions seek to cope with misinterpretations of the intent of Congress. A bungling bureaucracy has produced a tangled web of directives, guidelines, and rules that wreak legal havoc among institutions and usurp rights that hitherto many have believed to be the prerogative of these institutions.[20]

The easy way to assign blame is to put the whole burden on the bureaucracy, when as a matter of fact Congress must assume heavy responsibility, for in recent years it has moved more and more toward quick legislation inspired by political crisis; whereas its proper function is careful examination of the issues, sufficient public notification and hearings, thorough deliberation, and passage of laws that are in line with established principles of justice.

Dogmatic adherents to the time-honored principles of separation of church and state assume that, if the state becomes involved in religion to any degree, there will be repression, discrimination, and thought control. This theory is based largely on past history when governments had the power to advance one religion over another. Many defenders of complete separation of church and state approach the problem as if nothing has happened

---

[19]The Internal Revenue Service, for example, has taken for itself the right to exact penalties, issue prohibitions, and even to define the nature of a church—all without due process.

[20]Organizations such as the Center for Constitutional Studies at the Law School of Mercer University have done thorough research on court cases involving such rights and violations.

in the last hundred years that would modify their stance and change their priorities; as if World War II had never occurred, with its vast social, economic, and political upheaval; as if Vatican II had never taken place, with its liberalizing and ecumenical commitment; as if traditional Judeo-Christian value systems had remained intact and active; as if Martin Luther King, Jr. had never preached "We shall overcome"; as if mass communication media had had no effect on the world and its manners and morals; and as if the awful threat of nuclear destruction did not exist. A kind of decadent dialogue has developed, while the real issues are not being discussed.

The controversy over prayer and Bible-reading in the schools, for example, has engendered sharp and bitter debate, but neither opponents nor proponents are coming to grips with the deeper issues. It is doubtful whether the opponents have much evidence from past history that, if Bible-reading and prayer are allowed, the "wall of separation" will crumble and come tumbling down; it is just as doubtful that the claims of those who wish to retain Bible-reading and prayer in the public schools have any greater evidential support. Bible-reading and prayer in themselves have no mystic power or efficacy, and certainly a few moments of both will not bring about a revival of religion.

SECULARIZING PRESSURES ON EDUCATION

The deeper issue at stake is the answer to the question, How shall parents who wish to do so bring up their children in the fear and admonition of the Lord, in loyalty to the teachings of Christ, and in reverence for and obedience to the Bible? This could be the most important question that the Christian college will attempt to answer in this generation. Several important changes in American society have occurred that should challenge all Christians in America and that could not have been foreseen by the writers of the Bill of Rights, who lived in a time when Christianity was the dominant force in America. The impact of these major changes is only now coming to be recognized as a most serious challenge to the church and to institutions of the church.

The first of these changes is the rapid development of public education and the equally rapid decline in enrollment in private schools, which have been for the most part church-founded and church-oriented. The school-age population shift at all levels has been dramatic. As late as 1950, more than half the students enrolled in colleges and universities in the United States were in the private sector; today fewer than 20 percent are. Until the early part of the twentieth century, private high schools flourished in the South; most of them were church-related, many receiving indirect and direct public monies. Noteworthy also is the fact that many public schools in the South were controlled by white Protestant churchmen. There is a great deal of truth in the observation of an astute layman who said, "For a long time, most of our students were educated in two types of parochial schools: the Catholic parochial schools, supported by the Catholics, and the Protestant parochial schools, supported in many instances by the state."

A second great force at work was the steady secularization of American thought and culture, which became dominant throughout all public education just at the time when the school population shifted in this direction.

A third major development has been the decline of wealth available for charitable purposes. The advance of social concern, with the corresponding growth of government service programs (particularly in the areas of health, education, and welfare), has required such increases in taxation that the vast private wealth that once supported education, the arts, and scientific research may never again be available—nor should it be, if the price to be paid is human want, misery, deprivation, unequal opportunity, oppression, and injustice. Other government priorities such as national defense, foreign aid, space exploration, and subsidies to industry and agriculture have all greatly increased the tax burden and have made the cost of maintaining church-related schools almost prohibitive, both for a sponsoring denomination and for parent-patrons.

Some are laying a great burden upon the church and the home, but even under the most optimistic conditions, these institutions have very little real chance to serve as centers for religious instruction against the massive materialism of general education. Parents who have deep religious convictions and commitments are burdened by the almost complete isolation of the child from religious values. Past influence of the family and the church has steadily eroded.

Changed social conditions, the necessity in many families for both parents to be breadwinners, the increasing divorce rate, and new "educational forces" that have invaded the home, particularly through television, create special problems. Further to exacerbate the situation comes the serious modification of the rights that parents once exercised in the sanctity of their homes. The family is told that it is responsible for much of the current dilemma because of lack of discipline; yet, the law makes it possible for a thirteen-year-old girl to receive instruction in birth control, receive free birth-control medication or devices, or have an abortion—all without the knowledge and consent of her parents. Moreover, there is abundant evidence that sex education—which in itself has many positive possibilities— is often presented as far from neutral on what for Christians is a critical moral problem. One of the most pitiable developments has been the compromising of Christian moral principles by parents who have hoped that, in so doing, they could maintain some kind of relationship with their children. In many cases parents have ended by losing both their religion and their children.

Moreover, the church through its Sunday schools is proving far less than adequate. During the past fifty years, mainline churches overall have spent billions of dollars in developing large educational plants, modeled largely after the public school system, and have produced curricula appropriating much of the latest educational jargon in both the philosophy and methodology. Some classrooms in these educational plants are used, for the most part, only once or twice on Sunday. Even the most conscientious Sunday school teachers generally find themselves with only twenty to thirty minutes per week of actual teaching time. Even under optimum conditions, therefore, the religious instruction received by a child at home and in the church cannot offset the pressures generated by hours of secular instruction all week long in the school that the child is required to attend.

An alternative is a church-related school, but as has been pointed out, these exist now in fast-diminishing proportion to public schools. Such an option is not only a matter of simple justice in a democratic society but is also a viable means of generating reform in public education. Having affirmed, as a genius of the American social order, pluralism in almost every aspect of life—a pluralism that emerged from and was nurtured by a dual system of private and public education—this nation can hardly justify a monolithic structure of education, with the inevitable bureaucracy and ever-tightening tentacles of government control, using such powerful pressures as tax-exemption status, teacher certification, regulations on food and health services, safety precautions, equipment (for example, for the handicapped), and quotas.

Many religious parents of necessity send their children to the public schools, where the subjective aspect of religion has been by law (and rightly) prohibited as subject matter in general education. However, to distort science, for example, by omitting any mention that there has ever been a religious view of creation, and to distort history by failing to mention that there has been a religious dimension to the entire cultural heritage, is actually to present a false picture and to provide a faulty and incomplete education.

The central problem, one which cries for a solution, is the failure to transmit religious and societal values, even in an objective way. No one, surely, can argue against the plain fact that the highest values known had their origin in religion. The courts have made it clear that, in a pluralistic society, the government cannot support in its schools any value system that is religious in origin. In practice, the stance of public education has become value-neutrality. Actually there is no such thing as value-free instruction. What is omitted is thereby mutely declared to be of little importance. The result is a secular value system that has no reference to God; therefore, whatever approach it may make to moral instruction is relative.[21]

Essentially three questions are raised here: *Cultural*—Should state schools present the objective aspects of religion as part of the obligation to transmit to all students the complete knowledge and wisdom of the ages, a large portion of which is religious? *Political*—Is there support for revival and maintenance of free choice through a viable dual system of education? and *Economic*—How can a dual system be financed under present social conditions? It is becoming more and more difficult to comprehend how the present situation can continue without doing violence both to the "free exercise" and to the "no establishment" clauses of the First Amendment. The

---

[21]The concept *moral,* according to Plato, included courage, temperance, and justice. The word *moral* in the present day does not always enjoy that high definition, for the most part being relegated to matters of sex and social customs.

fact that secularization of the concept of law has been almost universally overlooked demonstrates a weakness in liberal arts education. Colleges and universities, both public and private, should do some earnest soul-searching about their responsibility, asking why so little attention has been paid to this crisis. No longer are the right questions being asked; often no questions are being asked at all.

ROLE OF CHRISTIAN HIGHER EDUCATION

Because the deepening crisis in the public sector of education is having such far-reaching consequences, Christian colleges and universities are almost compelled to step into the breach, for it is precisely in these institutions that the larger questions can be freely raised and debated without strictures or limitations on religious implications.

There are difficulties, to be sure. One is a great absence of familiarity, even among faculty, with both the cultural and religious heritage, particularly those writings that give the highest view of virtue and knowledge. The ever-increasing flow of technical knowledge, with the corresponding decrease in the study of liberal arts, poses a serious problem in that many faculty members as well as students are ill prepared for fruitful discussions on matters of philosophical import. One practical answer to this deficiency would be voluntary seminars in which those faculty members with traditional liberal arts training and those with more technical knowledge might share their resources and thus prepare one another through insights from their various disciplines to answer the kinds of questions that may arise in their classes.

Raising the questions is important, and even more significant is the observation that only in a church-related institution with a stated Christian purpose do teachers have the freedom to advocate Christian answers—not as indoctrination but as a demonstration that men and women of faith have credibility as well in the fields of scholarship and practical problem solving. Instructors are free in such a setting to show that revelation as a way of knowing[22] is just as intellectually respectable in its own realm as scientific data are in the areas of life where science reigns.

---

[22]Cf. Berdyaev's "conscious quest," Sinnott's "instinctive feeling," and Niebuhr's "divine disclosure of meaning in history and life."

Students should be considering, with help from informed and committed Christian faculty, such questions as the following:

1. Although not all good and just laws have had their origin in a religious view of man, ultimately can laws remain good and just by standards that are merely relative? Is law ever justified in limiting itself to man's current environment and to that which arises out of his psychological being, ruling out transcendent absolutes?

2. Is it feasible to try to achieve or evaluate just laws without reference to the vast cultural heritage of the best human thought about justice?

3. What should be the proper relationship between church and state? How can present tensions be eased? Have Bill of Rights protections of the church and institutions of the church been eroded, and if so, how can they be restored? What reforms can be effected in those aspects of public policy that affect religion and religious values?[23]

4. What changes in curriculum, textbooks, and teacher preparation can be made in order to provide all public school students with objective but convincing awareness that there has been and is now for many people a religious conviction about life that is intellectually tenable, widely accepted, and firmly motivating?

5. Since the Judeo-Christian tradition is disclaimed by the courts and the public schools, what basis can there be for such moral values as those that undergird responsible citizenship? How can these values be lawfully inculcated in the public schools so that people will learn to will what is right and just?

6. As nations are confronted with nuclear holocaust and the possibility of total destruction of the planet, what new world dimension must citizenship assume?

The necessity for international law was recognized by the ancients, and in more recent times, we have sought to give structure to world govern-

---

[23]This and several other short passages in this chapter have been adapted from a speech (in manuscript) by Ben C. Fisher entitled "Crisis in Canaan."

ment—earlier in the League of Nations, and now in the United Nations. However, people who are not good citizens of their own country, with all that that designation implies, are not likely to possess the insights and moral courage that will enable them to see the eventual necessity for world government, which is the only way to peace and to social and economic justice. Thus one of the greatest challenges for the Christian university in today's world is to advance the idea and ideals of responsible world government. The choice is between this and annihilation.

Some of the broader lessons to be learned from history are these: (1) that humanity's best periods, both ancient and modern, have been under democratic rather than despotic rule; (2) that societies which have achieved democracy in any measure have demonstrated that freedom comes slowly and at great sacrifice and is lost quickly unless there is perpetual vigilance; (3) that democracy, in order to flourish and be productive, must assume a citizenry of high moral character and integrity, without which law and justice cannot be enforced; (4) that the demise of a democratic state is more often the result of inward decay than of outward assault;[24] (5) that no society can long exist without just laws; and (6) that law functions best with the consent of the governed.[25] These are some of the major truths of which students need to be made aware.

The hope of achieving justice has ever been a high concept. Rigidity in the making, interpretation, and application of law can rob both people and institutions of former freedoms; however, the fault is not in the law per se but in our forgetting that both justice and judgment are not properties of law but qualities of character that prompt people to act rightly without fear, coercion, or hope of reward. The only remedy that can free a country from the inconsistencies and tyranny of modern bureaucracy is the state of mind that causes men and women to do the good and the right because they find joy in doing it. Justice is never static. Justice is acting justly.

---

[24]See Gibbon's *Decline and Fall of the Roman Empire,* Will and Ariel Durant's *Story of Civilization,* and Arnold Toynbee's *Study of History.*

[25]Even those (such as Hobbes) who defend despotic government maintain that the people must be protected by law.

The high view of law has always assumed, from ancient to modern times, not only that bad rulers cannot make good laws, but that even good laws have little or no meaning apart from the character of a citizenry that understands both the necessity and the benefits of an orderly society. In *Nicomachean Ethics,* book 5, Aristotle says, "We see that all men mean by justice that kind of state of character which makes people disposed to do what is just and makes them act justly and wish for what is just."[26] Both Plato and Aristotle would agree that, if men and women wish to sustain a government in which the habit of participation will prevail, they must be courageous, temperate, self-disciplined, and eager to seek wisdom. In other words, even good laws do not make good people; good people make good laws and obey them because they believe that such laws are necessary for the common welfare. While the Greeks were dedicated to personal freedom, they also recognized the extent to which individuals must limit their own rights in favor of the good of the community.

In this age of litigation, what is needed from a Christian university is graduates who have studied liberal arts under committed Christian teachers and have thus acquired a sound understanding of the complex concept of justice; graduates who will obey law for the right reasons and maintain a critical and sustained interest in making law reflect justice; above all, graduates who follow Christ in his admonition and his living, rendering unto Caesar the things that are Caesar's and unto God the things that are God's.

---

[26]Aristotle, *Nicomachean Ethics,* vol.9 of *Great Books,* 376.

CHAPTER 10

The Nature of Freedom

O God . . . whose service is perfect freedom. . . .
—BOOK OF COMMON PRAYER

Freedom is a fragile and intangible thing. It is as strong as steel and yet delicate as china. It can be infringed upon by a gesture. It can withstand the assault of armies, but it can just as surely be destroyed by one human voice.

One of the cries most often heard in the modern world is a call for "freedom," particularly civil or political freedom. When armies march, under whatever political ideology, they lay claim to the motivation of freeing captives. This was the cry of Lenin, of Mussolini, and of Hitler. Castro freed people from Yankee imperialism. Idi Amin promised freedom to the people of Uganda. The United States has sent armies halfway round the world and has suffered grievous losses in order to free people from oppression—more specifically, from Communism—so that now the two great world powers are arming day and night. Each lays claim to preserving human freedom.

The Christian university has an opportunity to raise old questions in new and meaningful ways. What has been past human experience in the pursuit of life, liberty, and happiness? What are the great documents that need to be reviewed and the great voices that need to be heard again? What is the difference between the individual's freedom and the expectations of the society and government in which he or she lives?

Although government is a central issue for our time, there is little evidence that college and university graduates have much knowledge of the long, tortuous, and sacrificial journey that Western man has traveled in pursuit of freedom. The period from the English Bill of Rights (1689) to the Universal Declaration of Human Rights (1948) represents almost three hundred years of struggle for human dignity. One fact is certain: whether it be a constitutional monarchy such as Great Britain or a representative democracy such as the United States, the independence of a government does not guarantee personal freedom. Although the Constitution of the United States is generally conceded to be one of the greatest documents guaranteeing human freedom, slavery was practiced under it, and the most basic human rights were denied to many of its people.

Western culture within the past three centuries has produced six great documents on human rights and the limits of government:

English Bill of Rights (1689)

Virginia Declaration of Rights (1776)

Declaration of Independence (1776)

French Declaration of the Rights of Man and of the Citizen (1789)

Charter of the United Nations (1945)

Universal Declaration of Human Rights (United Nations General Assembly, 1948)

At no time, under any government, have all the ideals mentioned in these documents been realized. From the English Bill of Rights (which in the main was addressed to limiting the power of the English monarch, giving rights to the nobility and establishing the sovereignty of Parliament) to the Universal Declaration of Human Rights there has been a steadily broadening view of human dignity, security, and freedom. What is suggested by this relatively brief period in history is that the conflict between the ideal and the actual will be a continuing problem.

Moreover, society is ever confronted with the problem of what is too much and what is too little government. How is the freedom of the individual to be weighed against the good of society, and what are the limits to which society can go in restricting the God-given (or natural) rights of an individual?

Notice that the meaning of *freedom* and *liberty* is not always clear, for the words have been used in such a variety of contexts that, for many, their meaning has become obscured.[1] In many instances, the words seem to have taken on an almost mythical character, as if they were absolutes to be claimed by the individual. Here the existentialists are right: whether viewed from a material or transcendent perspective, each one of us is born to a world of limitations. We did not ask to be born, but we are thrust into the world and have absolutely no control over either our entrance into life or our exit. We may wish to live, but we most certainly shall die; we have no choice as to race, natural endowments, or the social condition of our parents; most important of all, death is absolute. Recognizing these limitations could have a substantive effect on overinflated egos and expectations.

Historically, from the Greeks to the present day, there has been the idea of natural freedom; that is, individuals born into the world have the right to live, to eat, to clothe and shelter themselves, to reproduce their kind, and to seek what satisfaction they may find. This idea is fully articulated in the preamble to the American Constitution.

Both Hobbes and Locke would say, however, that people even in their natural state could never be completely independent, since they are always subject to the unpredictable forces of nature. In the civilized state, their freedom is limited also by man-made laws.

Not only laws but the very structure of society in a given era may have an enormous effect on human freedom. Adam Smith in *The Wealth of Nations* could not possibly have foreseen that, when he wrote his essay "Di-

---

[1] In order to approach this problem in its proper historical context in the area of civil liberties and jurisprudence, the following works could be helpful: Aristotle, *The Nicomachean Ethics* and *The Athenian Constitution;* Hobbes, *Leviathan;* Locke, *An Essay concerning Human Understanding;* Montesquieu, *The Spirit of Laws;* Kant, *The Science of Right;* John Stuart Mill, *On Liberty;* Hegel, *The Philosophy of Right;* Dostoevsky, *The Brothers Karamazov;* and the Constitution of the United States.

vision of Labor," the stage was being set for what was to become a powerful influence in limiting individual initiative and development. Smith pointed out that one man making nails might make a thousand nails a day, but that if four men who were engaged in making nails should divide the labor, each specializing in one part of the process, they could more than double the production that could be expected of four men individually. Thus at the same time that the great universities—first in Europe, then in the United States—were turning to research and narrow specialization in all fields, specialization in industry found its greatest success when Henry Ford introduced the assembly line, where individuals perform the same unending task, day in and day out, with resultant damage to the workers forever satirized in one of Charlie Chaplin's greatest movies.

Specialization of knowledge and of labor has produced a deadening effect on imagination. Aristotle observed in his treatise *Poetics* that the poet's function is not merely to describe what has already taken place but to imagine what might happen in the future. In the area of aesthetics, imagination has been the basis for art, literature, and architecture. In pure science and even in the practical fields, it has been the basis for progress. Had not Michael Faraday imaginatively observed the reaction of a needle's floating on water when it was exposed to a magnet, the electric generator and the electric motor might never have been developed. Faraday was a learned scientist; on the other hand, Thomas Edison was a telegrapher without formal education. The common tie between the two was not only observation but creative imagination.

It should be noted that industry is becoming more aware of the drawbacks of overspecialization and in some cases is breaking the monotony of the assembly line by training workers to do several tasks and alternating their work assignments. Moreover, companies in some instances are paying for special courses in the humanities for management. And higher education as a whole has been recognizing the problems of narrow specialization. The Christian university should seize upon this opportunity to insist that there are no fetters like the fetters of narrowness, absence of sensitivity, and dullness of imagination.

Another unseen and often unperceived limitation on human freedom is a lack of knowledge of the past. Partly as a result of overspecialization, ignorance of history looms large in contemporary culture. Cynics such as Hegel have maintained that "peoples and governments never learned anything from history or acted on principles deduced from it." If this statement is true, the task of education is even more formidable than had been supposed, because both persons and governments must be able to learn from the past. Whatever we know, apart from divine revelation, we learn from experience; the broadening of this experience is a primary function of education. If this were not possible, every single one of us would have to start from the beginning.

Indeed, one of humanity's greatest efforts has been to preserve the heritage of the ages. Human beings are the only creatures who, through their rational faculties, not only can preserve the past but can weigh it against the present and the future. In *History of the Peloponnesian War* Thucydides said that it was his desire to preserve "an exact knowledge of the past as an aid to the interpretation of the future, which in the course of human things must resemble if it does not reflect it." His high view of the usefulness of history is further reflected in his statement, "I have written my work, not as an essay which is to win the applause of the moment, but as a possession for all time."[2] Hegel himself, paradoxically, put his thoughts in writing—presumably for the edification of posterity in spite of his cynicism; his influence, particularly on dialectical materialism, disproves his own theory that government leaders cannot be affected by the past. So great is human respect for the past that during World War II both the Nazis and the Allies were loath to destroy the great museums, libraries, and cathedrals.

The stimulus to imagination that can be furnished by a knowledge of past human accomplishment is so valuable that there can be no substitute for it. Recent attempts to make curricula "relevant" have impoverished students by allowing the best of past human thought to be crowded out of the courses of study. Christian universities do a service to freedom of thought by taking steps to restore a proper balance.

A study of the past will reveal rich Greek resources on the concept of freedom. The Greeks early understood that freedom has a price. This was

---

[2]Thucydides, *History of the Peloponnesian War*, vol. 6 of *Great Books*, 354.

the theme of the myth of Prometheus, who stole fire from the gods. Aeschylus enlarged the ancient myth so that his hero stole not only fire but, symbolically, knowledge and wisdom as well and was forever punished as a consequence.

> Lo, I am he
> Who, darkly hiding in a fennel reed
> Fountains of fire, so secretly purloined
> And gave to be the teacher of all arts
> And giver of all good to mortal men.
> And now this forfeit for my sin I pay,
> Thus lodged in fetters under the bare sky.[3]

No more poignant document on freedom has been penned than *Prometheus Bound*. This legend illustrates the great difference between the Christian view and that of Greek culture. The free will that the Jewish and Christian God embodied in the creation of man stands in sharp contrast to the independence that Prometheus had to obtain by stealth and at great sacrifice.

In Greek poetry and drama, fate held inexorable sway over the tragic hero. Oedipus was doomed to kill his father, and Orestes his mother. Yet even within this necessity there was still left some choice. The gods did not—or could not—prevent Prometheus from stealing the fire, although Zeus could and did punish him. The myth of Sisyphus, revived by Camus in modern times, is a similar illustration of the fact that Greek mythology left individuals some limited room for attainment and for acceptance of their fate. However, man's great limitation, as the Greeks saw it, was that he had to wrest from the gods whatever achievement he wished to attempt. The gods were at worst hostile to his ambitions, and at best indifferent.

Thus it is on an individual's own choice that the problem of freedom focuses, even in the Greek view, and much more so for the Hebrew and the Christian. Even though we are limited—by heredity, by environment, by death—our freedom consists in our admittedly restricted power of choice.

---

[3]Oates and Murphy, *Greek Literature in Translation*, 143.

Of all the obligations a Christian university faces in these times, none exceeds the responsibility for restating the Christian idea of freedom. The task will be a complicated one because it is inevitably bound up with the problem of good and evil. Tolstoy has pointed out that the problem of evil is a question for theology. Human responsibility to society is a question for law. The distinction between right and wrong is a question for ethics. The influence of individuals' past actions in regard to freedom is a question for history.

The above categories listed by Tolstoy outline the breadth of the problem of freedom, which should be a challenge to every area of university thought. The departments of philosophy and religion, in particular, should reexamine freedom in the light of fate, necessity, free will, Providence, and what have been termed "natural rights."

All civilizations have developed some high concepts of right and wrong—of justice and kindness as against injustice and unconcern. Certainly an important enforcer of these concepts has been the hope of reward and the fear of punishment, if not by God, then at least by society. Such hope and fear are strongly suggested in the Old Testament, and in the New Testament frequent mention is made of rewards for the faithful.

But Jesus brought a whole new dimension to the ethical perspective of the Christian, who is to do the right thing out of a love of God and love of neighbor and in so doing is to lift righteousness and ethical concern above the dead legalism of either the fear of punishment or the hope of reward. In this free atmosphere right is for right's sake, love is for love's sake, concern is for concern's sake, and all are for God's sake.

In Romans 6, 7, and 8, Paul speaks of three kinds of freedom: freedom from sin (6:18)—not only from the sins of the flesh, but freedom from missing the mark with one's life (this is the central meaning of hamartia); freedom from law (7:6)—which lifted the terrible burden of the *shalt not*s of the Ten Commandments and the endless rules and rituals of the Pharisees; and freedom from death (8:2). If human beings are alone, there is indeed no exit; but we are not alone. While our past is irretrievable, in Jesus Christ we lay claim to the future.

Among the fundamental precepts of the early Christian community was that of freedom, which was conceived to be a paradox: persons are free only as they are willing to be bound to the highest ideal they know. Freedom then takes the form of making a choice (a theme again finding expression in existential philosophy).

This one free choice a person has: his or her allegiance. Only when the decision to become the bondservant of Christ has been made does one have the power to become free. One cannot *will* freedom; one receives it as a gift. Nor, without help, is one free, even to make the right choices in the daily decisions that the Christian in the world has to make. Paul testifies to this very clearly in Romans 7:19: "For the good that I would, I do not: but the evil which I would not, that I do."

But Christians are not only free *from* something; they are free *for* something. Therefore their freedom is inextricably bound by responsibility. Whatever the individual does, either as a personal or communal act, must never be done either at the expense of Christ's teachings or to the detriment of a neighbor. Out of this concept the idea of freedom is developed both for the transmission of knowledge and for the conduct of the Christian community of faith and learning.

One needs to be reminded that, for the early Christian, there were no constitutional guarantees, no statutory protection, no court of appeal, and no authority to whom one could turn for help. Christians were free because they were faithful beyond life unto death. Neither the threat of death nor the hope of earthly reward nor the infliction of torture could deter them. And thus it was that the humblest Christian, free or slave, could shake the foundations of the greatest empire the world had known. In our time Albert Camus said, in *Resistance, Rebellion, and Death*, that if Christians would stand up and speak up, they could change the world. In this era it is appropriate to raise the question whether Christians have come to view freedom as a natural right under law rather than as a gift from God, which only the steadfast conscience of a Christian can protect.

CHAPTER 11

Academic Freedom

It is essential to the health and vitality of a society that there be in it a point at which ideas can not only emerge, but can survive to be freely and completely examined.

—ROBERT H. EWING

The question of academic freedom has become a new challenge, particularly to those church-related institutions that wish to maintain strong ties with the denomination and that have developed a broad and comprehensive statement of Christian purpose and commitment. The classic statement of academic freedom and responsibility was issued in 1940 by the American Association of University Professors (AAUP). This is a pivotal educational document. Its felicity of expression and sense of proportion and balance have made it a literary as well as an educational achievement. However, at the time when this document was put together, administrators as well as faculty members participated in constructive dialogue. The great controversies of the fifties and sixties over governance, student rights, and institutional responsibilities lay in the future.

Several developments that could not have been foreseen at the time the 1940 statement was formulated have exerted an influence on the interpretation of academic freedom. Then the AAUP was a well-organized and committed voice for academic freedom. *When the AAUP chose to become largely a collective bargaining agent, its claim to be the sole arbiter in matters of academic freedom was considerably weakened.* There was a radical shift in emphasis from the statement as a whole to the rights of the individual. This shift was in keeping with the tenor of the times, but it had a chilling effect on the teacher's obligation to exercise responsibility in carrying out the stated purpose of the institution.

In order to achieve academic excellence, a unique system of accreditation has been developed in this country, with broad standards that assist each educational institution in measuring its progress toward excellence. The key to the accrediting procedure is the institution's statement of purpose. The preamble to the *Standards* set forth by the Southern Association of Colleges and Schools states that *the rights of an institution to fulfill the purposes for which it was founded are held to be incontestable.* Every other standard must be weighed and measured in the light of the stated purpose. Thus any application of the Statement of Principles of academic freedom must be weighed against the overall statement of purpose of each institution.

When the 1940 Statement of Principles was issued, it was noted that those institutions having special religious requirements should put these guidelines in writing and make them available to faculty members at the time of employment. However, this modification was subsequently dropped, and its omission has created in some cases special problems for the church-related college or university.

A major innovation that has had many positive aspects is the development of the faculty senate, which in theory and practice has given faculties a larger voice in recommending educational policies. This new voice, however, has not always spoken with the proper understanding of its role. The high-sounding faculty senate sometimes has seemed to forget that, unlike the ancient Roman Senate or the United States Senate, its function is not legislative. To this degree the faculty senate has occasionally overlooked its limitations within the charter of the institution. It also sometimes has found itself so consumed with individual rights that overall responsibilities to the general purpose of the institution are at least momentarily lost.

The faculty senate is not a policy-making body; policy is the responsibility of the trustees. While the faculty has every right—and even an obligation—to make recommendations concerning policy, the court of last resort must be the trustees. While wise trustees should consider the suggestions of the faculty senate, it is the board of trustees who must make the final decisions in matters of tenure, employment, dismissals, and all other administrative matters and who must challenge any violation of the purpose of the institution.

In other developments, the Civil Rights Act and subsequent court decisions concerning the rights of individuals have created a whole series of new problems for both public and private institutions. Most public and many private colleges and universities have abandoned all attempts to guide student conduct, either on or off campus, and the traditional concept of the college standing in loco parentis in many cases has been pronounced dead.[1] Some in public as well as private schools feel that the surrender of all dormitory regulations and the abandonment of any attempt to transmit moral and ethical values as a part of the instructional process are partly to blame for the present chaos in American education and civil life.

A Christian university is bound to its commitment of purpose, which holds that character is the key to conduct and that conduct of both students and faculty should balance freedom with ultimate responsibility. Accord-

---

[1]Derek Bok, *Beyond the Ivory Tower: Social Responsibilities of the Modern University* (Cambridge: Harvard University Press, 1982) 31, 122, has gone as far as to say that at Harvard the matter of character as a criterion for employment of faculty is no longer considered.

> The proper function of a university is to choose for its faculty those persons who are best qualified to perform the educational and scholarly tasks for which they are hired, provided they are capable of observing the elementary standards of conduct essential to the welfare and safety of an academic community. The task of judging those who have transgressed against society is a separate responsibility that should be left to the public authorities, who are better equipped to discharge this function properly. . . . Even with the awakening interest in ethics, no research university could hope to reinstitute character as a basis for appointments. The criterion is simply too susceptible to abuse, too vague, too remote from the primary commitment to learning and discovery.

ing to the section of the 1940 Statement of Principles that deals with the college or university teacher:

> When he speaks or writes as a citizen, he should be free from institutional censorship or discipline, but his special position in the community imposes special obligations. As a man of learning and an educational officer, he should remember that the public may judge his profession and his institution by his utterances. Hence he should at all times be accurate, should exercise appropriate restraint, should show respect for the opinions of others, and should make every effort to indicate that he is not an institutional spokesman.[2]

To suppose that teachers in a Christian college or university would conduct themselves as if they were not bound by their own and their institution's Christian commitment, or that their concept of freedom would match that of a teacher in a secular institution, is utterly naive. Whether they are recommending books for their courses, writing speeches, or engaging in publication, teachers in a Christian college or university must make their first priority reflecting the purpose of the institution, to which purpose they have voluntarily committed their career. Thus Christian teachers find their freedom in faithfulness, becoming the bondservants of Christian commitment.

---

[2]"1940 Statement of Principles," *AAUP Policy Documents and Reports* (Washington, D.C.: American Association of University Professors, 1977) 2.

CHAPTER 12

The Trustee

All power is a trust; . . . we are accountable for its exercise.
—BENJAMIN DISRAELI

If trusteeship has ever been a merely honorary position, it certainly is so no longer. Responsible trusteeship calls for time, thought, and sometimes agonizing decisions, as well as considerable preparation and concern. Never has it been more important for trustees to have a clear understanding of their duties and responsibilities and to keep abreast of changes in higher education at large.

Since the trustees have ultimate accountability for a college or university, they must assure that it is properly performing its mission, that it has established appropriate standards, and that its faculty and facilities are, insofar as possible, adequate to the assigned task. Trustees must concern themselves with whether or not the various groups within the institution—the administration, faculty, and students—are working harmoniously together and whether, on the issues that affect each particular group, policies and procedures exist through which the voice of that group can be heard.

Moreover, the trustee of a Christian college or university is not just the trustee of an educational institution; he or she is the trustee of a *Christian* educational institution, which has a unique mission in the world. Consequently, such a trustee has an exceptionally grave duty to see to it that his or her institution, which is offering services in the name of Christ, offers them on the highest possible level. Any responsible institution serving society should, of course, do its best; but the Christian institution has a special commitment, as well as special problems in maintaining a place of service in a society that seems to be more and more alien to Christian virtues and values.

PRINCIPAL PURPOSES

The primary responsibility of trustees is to safeguard the purposes for which the institution they represent was founded. These purposes are, in the case of the Christian college, a "response to the mandate of our Lord to know and to teach the truth, and to the clear intent of the Scriptures that God shall not be left without a witness to the minds of his children."[1]

The institutional statement of purpose arises out of the beliefs that give the Christian college its reason for being and make its impact unique, "with no conflict between the life of faith and the life of inquiry."[2] Both the American Association of University Professors and the general accrediting agencies recognize that every school has a right to carry out the purposes for which it was founded. In the case of the Christian college, this is not only a right but a divine obligation.

Sometimes difficulties arise when trustees assume that, as long as the statement of Christian purpose is printed in the catalogue or appears in the minutes of the board, nothing more is required. The temptation has been and continues to be to place such emphasis on the educational objectives that Christian purpose and denominational service are neglected to a point where many people see little or no difference between church-related and

---

[1]"Our Covenant Relationship," in *Reaffirmations,* adopted by the Association of Southern Baptist Colleges and Schools, 12 June 1976, National Colloquium on Christian Education (Nashville TN: Education Commission of the Southern Baptist Convention, 1976).

[2]Statement of Purpose, *Trustee Handbook* (Buies Creek NC: Campbell University, 1984) vii.

public institutions. Indeed, educational objectives must be met. Without accreditation a college does not have any academic standing. There would be nothing so contradictory as to offer second-rate education under the guise of Christian piety. But Christian institutions should never be satisfied by meeting only minimum standards. The ultimate objective should be to offer superior services plus Christian concern for each person to whom they minister.

Covenants and statements of purpose have little meaning unless they become active goals and guidelines for the total program of the college. They erode most quickly when they are not reflected in the hiring of faculty and other personnel and when they are not reflected in the admissions policy and in the total teaching program. At the time of employment, each teacher, who should already have had verbal explanations, ought to be handed in writing (in addition to the terms of the contract, rank, salary, fringe benefits, advancement provisions, conditions for tenure, retirement policies, teaching load, channels for grievance, and so forth) a statement of the purposes, aims, and objectives of the college or university. Trustees have a continuing responsibility to see that, throughout the institution, only those persons are employed who can live within the stated purpose.

The most important document, therefore, to be developed at any college or university is a clear, cohesive, and concise statement of purpose. This declaration, required by every regional accrediting agency, is the standard by which all programs and activities of the institution are judged when at regular intervals the institution is professionally evaluated. The integrity of the college is measured by its conscientious endeavor to fulfill its stated purpose.[3] A study by Earl J. McGrath, further substantiated by John Minter Associates, indicates that church-related institutions that have articulated a clear-cut statement of Christian purpose and denominational commitment have fared better both in student enrollment and in financial

---

[3]*Standards of the College Delegate Assembly of the Southern Association of Colleges and Schools* (Atlanta GA: Commission on Colleges, Southern Association of Colleges and Schools, 1979) 1.

support than those schools that have been either apologetic or very weak about their church-relatedness.[4]

Trustees are responsible for seeing to it that the institution's expectations of all personnel have been stated in writing and placed in the hands of each employee, including clearly outlined procedural due process for dismissal. Students' relationship with the college or university should likewise be understood to be contractual: prior to each student's enrollment, he or she should be furnished rules and regulations in writing; procedural due process should be made unmistakably clear, and in case of dismissal for disciplinary reasons should be followed to the letter, with stated charges, a fair open hearing, and the privilege of counsel. In recent years, an increasing number of students and faculty have sought redress through the courts, and in a few cases have sued individual board members. The best way to ensure the carrying out of an institution's purpose is by preventive action and by the creation of a climate where disruption is not likely to occur.

After the primary task of safeguarding purpose, the next most important role of the trustee is in the election of a president, if that duty falls within the trustee's term of office. In American higher education the role of the chief executive is such that success or failure of the institution, to a large degree, depends upon the quality and integrity of presidential leadership. While trustees will make the final decision, others who are related to the institution—faculty, students, and alumni—should be given a real voice in the selection of the chief officer. Whatever method is used, the importance of vitally involving the faculty, particularly, is incontestable.

Other responsibilities of trustees include the following:

managing all funds and properties under sound fiscal practices;

approving all policies under which the college or university operates;

raising funds;

making sure that the budget accurately mirrors the educational aims and objectives of the institution;

planning for future growth and development;

---

[4]Earl J. McGrath, *Study of Southern Baptist Colleges and Universities, 1976-1977* (Nashville TN: Education Commission of the Southern Baptist Convention, 1977) 19-20.

handling problems of students and faculty governance and academic freedom;

studying ways and means to undergird the academic program and meet accreditation standards;

maintaining good public relations;

providing suitable services to the constituency and the community;

seeing that federal regulations and guidelines are met;

protecting the institution from pressure groups (without or within) who would exert force not in keeping with the stated purpose of the college;

handling grievances that have not been satisfactorily settled under procedures established by the administration;

and acting as a court of last resort in dealing with both the institution and the constituency.

Trustees' increasing legal responsibility and "personal vulnerability" have been made clear in a report published by the American Association for Higher Education.

> Recent court cases make it clear that the individual trustees can be held accountable and may be sued in a court of law for institutional debts, personal or professional injury to any campus personnel, or bad management of any sort. In addition, the trustee can no longer plead absence from a board meeting or ignorance about what is going on in the institution as a defense against responsibility.[5]

Some of the legal problems that continue to multiply, both from within the institution and from outside forces, relate to student admissions, student discipline, academic freedom, use of publicly funded facilities, and religious preference in employment practices. Federal legislation and guidelines are placing ever more serious restrictions on the traditional inherent freedom of general education. The institution's legal counsel should keep abreast of these matters and keep the board informed.

For the making of wise decisions, channels should be devised to assure the genuine involvement of all institutional components: the governing

---

[5]Robert M. Hendrickson and Ronald Scott Mangum, *Governing Board and Administration Liability,* ERIC Higher Education Research Report No. 9 (Washington D.C.: American Association for Higher Education, 1977) 11.

board, administration, faculty, students, and in some cases, alumni. But the trustees alone must assume the responsibility for establishing policies and for recording, publishing, and making known these policies to parties concerned.

DELICACY OF CAMPUS RELATIONSHIPS

Once the broad policies have been established, implementation should be turned over to the president and his administrative staff. Trustees assist, guide, and evaluate, but *"the board of trustees is a legislative, not an executive body, whose primary responsibility is the determination of policy.* This means most importantly that the board's function is not administrative. . . . Execution of policy must be scrupulously left in the hands of the president."[6]

Well-defined principles govern the relationship between the trustee and the president. Because of the unique position of responsibility that the president of a college holds and because the president reports directly for the institution to the board of trustees, he or she must be clearly recognized by all as the one responsible for carrying out the policies of the board. It is of the greatest importance that the president not be bypassed either deliberately or thoughtlessly. "Nothing will make an institution quiver to its foundations more quickly than evidence or rumor that the board relies more confidently upon someone else than it relies upon the president."[7] The best of institutional presidents will be a much better administrative officer with the full support of the board. Occasional expressions of appreciation from individual board members and from the board as a whole will lighten the burden of the chief executive and make him or her a more secure and more productive person.

Conversely, the necessity for the president's honest sharing of full information with the board can scarcely be overemphasized; for the trustees, though they determine policy, look to the president, staff, and faculty for

---

[6]Myron F. Wicke, *Handbook for Trustees,* Studies in Christian Higher Education, No. 5 (Nashville TN: Board of Education, Methodist Church, 1962) 22.

[7]Harold W. Stoke, *The American College President* (New York: Harper & Row, Publishers, 1959) 77.

guidance. The administration owes to the trustees a clear-cut view of the institutional operation, carefully planned board and committee meetings with sufficient advance information about the agenda, regular financial statements including at least a quarterly balance sheet, aggressive leadership in long-range planning and in problem solving, and promptness and integrity in reporting the bad news as well as the good.

A good trustee should remain friendly, concerned, and interested in all institutional personnel, not just the president. Structured communication and relationships should exist (committee work, social occasions such as receptions, and so on), but there is an appropriate and impersonal distance that the nature of the office demands that the trustee observe. There are some dangers in seeking out individual faculty members, unless they are charged with some specific function or responsibility. There is a fine line between respect and disqualifying friendship—a line that may become a sensitive matter where friendships have already existed, but in this case the well-being of the institution must take precedence. Trustees may have to serve sometime as a court of last resort, and for that reason the quality of fellowship that should be encouraged is that which could not eventually develop into a conflict of interest. Rarely is it wise for a trustee to press for particular persons to be appointed, promoted, or discharged. He should always keep in mind that a trustee works through the administration, which should keep him fully informed at all times.

Moreover, all policy decisions should be made by the board as a whole. The various trustees, to be sure, should act, think, and work as individuals with no "ax to grind"—theological, denominational, administrative, or financial—voting not as representatives, emissaries, or delegates with even the appearance of a conflict of interest but as informed persons according to their knowledge, conscience, and integrity. But when the board has made a decision, particularly on a controversial matter, it is wise to have only one spokesperson for the institution and to set forth a complete and frank statement giving the facts leading up to the action and the reasons for the board's decision. Secrecy after solution tends to magnify the situation and to do considerable harm, both to the institution and sometimes to the persons involved. If pressed by the media, individual trustees have a right to say, "I stand by the decision of the board and have no further comment at this time." The above statement in no way abridges the right of particular trustees to say whatever they want to say. It merely points out that they have a right to remain silent as well as to speak.

ASPECTS OF TRUSTEE RESPONSIBILITY

The trustee system for governing the educational process is uniquely American. Trustees of American colleges and universities are almost exclusively laymen rather than professional educators. "Education is not an exact science. Its experts can profit from the criticism and suggestions of intelligent laymen."[8] But if trustees are to act responsibly, their first task is to become informed in a rapidly changing and many times confused field. Management has become more complex, and finances more difficult. Educational goals and objectives are having to be restudied and redefined. Legal problems continue to multiply. A responsible board of trustees that keeps abreast can participate in the decision-making process and not merely approve recommendations that members really do not understand. Sometimes one hears the suggestion that a trustee ought not to be a rubber stamp; but unfortunately when trustees come on an institutional board with the sole objective of not being a rubber stamp and with little prior understanding of the purpose and problems of the institution, paradoxically they may become a rubber stamp that reads "No." From the youngest, most inexperienced to the oldest and wisest member of the board, gaining new knowledge, developing new insights, and pressing forward to meet the goals of the institution will be an ongoing process.

A large body of helpful literature has been developed, including books, monographs, periodicals, newsletters, and special studies. Much information will be sent out from the president's office. Professional organizations (like the national Association of Governing Boards, located in the nation's capital) provide workshops and produce special literature. Often the denomination or the institution itself sponsors orientation sessions for trustees. But the ultimate responsibility for understanding the purpose of the college, its goals, and its operation is always in the initiative of the in-

---

[8]Stoke, *American College President*, 72.

dividual trustee. Wanting to learn and taking the time that is necessary ought to be a part of the trust commitment. This does not mean that trustees will not look to the administration for guidance, recommendation, and the setting of goals, but it does mean that, if they merely give their stamp of approval without understanding the significance of these recommendations, they are never likely to give the zeal and enthusiasm that are necessary for implementation.

Another important aspect of trusteeship is, and always has been, a financial responsibility. Because Christian colleges must operate in the mainstream of higher education, they share many problems of higher education generally. In the field of finance, these include rising costs (for instruction, building, plant operation, and maintenance), inflation, and the need for more efficient management.

The tax structure has reduced considerably the income from corporations and individual donors, while public colleges and universities have made devastating inroads upon foundation and corporate giving. In many cases, a large single source of income for the church-related college, outside of student fees, is the sponsoring denomination, with whom tensions often arise. Anti-intellectualism has always been present in varying degrees in American society;[9] and to churches, a college is always a calculated risk, for an institution of higher learning will ever be on the frontiers of dialogue and discovery. While the tie that binds the college and the denomination together ought to be more substantive than that of money, the interdependence ought to be a sobering fact that will give impetus to the constant search by trustees for better understanding and more effective ways of serving. The primary relationship between the church-related college and its sponsor should not be a coercive one but a covenant, causing school and church to work together in freedom and faithfulness. Each has a vital contribution to make to the other, and both stand perpetually in need of spiritual renewal and a fresh sense of mission in today's world.

The financial plight of private higher education is so critical that the future of the American dual system of public and private sectors is threat-

---

[9]Richard Hofstadter, *Anti-Intellectualism in American Life* (New York: A. Knopf, 1963) 48-50.

ened. In order to help meet increasing financial needs, trustees themselves each year should make a personal gift to their institution, according to their means. Persons with a modest income should not be embarrassed because they cannot make large contributions, and those with wealth should not feel that their primary reason for being on the board is their ability to give. But in any approach to a corporation or foundation, one of the questions generally asked is, How well are the trustees, faculty, and alumni already responding to this need? Any time that the president can say that 100 percent of the board has made a contribution, his or her hand has been greatly strengthened. Someone has said that a good rule of thumb on giving is, No gift is so small that it will go unappreciated, or so large that others will be unnecessary.

In addition to giving personally, each trustee should seek to lead others to contribute. A good trustee is a chief instrument in long-range cultivation of all sources of income, particularly from individuals, corporations, and foundations. The board will also be concerned with the importance of wills and trusts.

There was a period when there was little argument with the proposition that one of the chief functions of a trustee was to give or get money. While that is still a high priority, active participation by individual trustees in recruitment of students is now equally important. If each board member would recruit at least two students each year (and find financial sponsors if necessary) this would help to produce considerable additional gross income without necessitating the addition of any new teaching personnel. Moreover, thousands of people are not interested in campaigns for buildings, endowments, current expenses, or debt retirement but get great joy and fulfillment out of assisting a particular student to get a college education. Said one trustee, "The easiest money to raise is scholarship money." Said another, who had attended a recruitment seminar, gone home immediately, recruited two top students, and solicited financial aid for them, "In all the years that I have been a trustee, I have never done anything that has given me more personal pleasure."

Concern for the welfare of students is a significant part of the trustee's commitment. As elementary as it may seem, there is need to be reminded that after all, the institution exists for the student. In a Christian university there is a responsibility

> to treat the student at all times as a person of worth; to instill in students a thirst for knowledge; to enable them to develop life goals; to help students to discriminate among values; and to encourage in them a Christian world view, responsible Christian citizenship, active participation in the life of their church, the development of a sense of vocational mission, . . . and a deeper commitment to Christ.[10]

While trustees, of course, are not expected to keep in their minds all the details that relate to the welfare of the student, they must keep in their hearts always a deep concern, not only to meet the student's physical needs (housing, food services, health and safety programs, and library, laboratory, and classroom facilities) but also to create an atmosphere conducive to learning and spiritual growth.

Moreover, there must be regular channels for voicing student opinion; students must know and trust these procedures; and the college or university must demonstrate that it will not only hear student opinion but study it seriously and, if possible, act upon it. Student rights and freedoms are to be respected, and student responsibilities clearly understood. One of the keys to preventing or containing disruption of a college or university is allowing and encouraging responsible student and faculty leadership to function. To see this happen might well be one of the most effective educational experiences in a student's college career.

PARTNERSHIP WITH FACULTY AND ADMINISTRATION

The relationship of the trustees to the faculty and staff is also crucial. All groups should have a clear understanding of their respective roles, both in scope and in limitations.

The lay system of trusteeship in American higher education has been productive because trustees have been wise enough to delegate authority and assign responsibilities to competent educators, especially in the areas that are primarily academic.[11] Although the trustees are responsible to see

---

[10]*Reaffirmations.*

[11]Gerald P. Burns, *Trustees in Higher Education: Their Function and Coordination* (N.p.: Independent College Funds of America, 1966) 90.

that the instructional program is effective in achieving not only accreditation but also the stated purpose of the institution, and although the trustees hold the power of review and final decision in matters of academic freedom and responsibility, they must leave teaching to the teacher in the same manner in which they leave administrative matters to the president.

But a much more meaningful relationship than merely that of employer and employee needs to exist between the board on the one hand and the faculty and administration on the other. The most productive educational situation always results from an effective partnership between the trustees, faculty, and administration.

In certain areas of mutual responsibility faculty members have primary concern: "curriculum, subject matter and methods of instruction, research, faculty status, and those aspects of student life which relate to the educational process."[12] A wise board will seek advice through the proper channels from the professional experts whom it has employed to carry out the academic program. Such a policy will build up morale, increase the feeling of solidarity within the academic family, and safeguard the democratic processes characteristic of American higher education. Moreover, faculty liaison in the selection of a new president is now universally recognized as being both right and necessary, although there are several possible approaches, and it must be understood that the final responsibility for the choice is solely that of the trustees.

Other areas in which trustees may wish faculty to have input, though perhaps not a vote, are long-range planning; use and development of physical plant, budgeting, selection of deans and other chief academic officers, and institutional relations with the public. There is general agreement that better lines of communication should be established between trustees and faculties and that, beyond mere communication, faculties should have an equitable and appropriate voice in policy-making through regular structured channels.

---

[12]American Association of University Professors, American Council on Education, and Association of Governing Boards of Universities and Colleges, *Statement on Government of Colleges and Universities,* Reprinted from AAUP Bulletin 52 (Winter 1966) (Washington, D.C.: American Association of University Professors, n.d.) 10.

Above all, the faculty and administrative staff need to feel that their needs are of concern to the trustees. Although many teachers in church-related colleges have a sense of mission that leads them to make financial sacrifices, worthy compensation is a major force for morale building on the campus and a necessary factor for maintaining the vitality of the institution. Teachers who are barely able to feed and clothe their families cannot give their best performance in the classroom. One of the best ways to recruit and retain faculty is to have the board demonstrate a real concern for the financial security and professional improvement of each teacher. Salary scales, housing provisions, and fringe benefits—such as various types of insurance, secretarial help, loans and emergency funds, moving expenses, retirement programs, and educational privileges for faculty and staff families—are important ways of adding greatly to the security and contentment of the college or university, and at relatively small cost.

Faculty may also need provisions for professional improvement: sabbatical leaves, leaves of absence for work on advanced degrees or other approved purposes, funds to attend meetings of professional learned societies, and library provisions for faculty research. Well-defined policies concerning teaching load, research, and administrative work will increase the effectiveness of teaching, make the work of the dean and president much easier, and strengthen morale. "The most important compensation of a faculty member is the opportunity to do pleasant and useful work under conditions that make it effective."[13]

Teaching, for the *good* teacher, has never been an easy task. It has never been a profession that has produced rich financial rewards, nor has the teacher been uplifted by praise and recognition, except (usually) at retirement. If, instead of receiving five hundred letters in a bound volume at the time of retirement, teachers receive a few of these each year, they will doubtless approach their work with greater joy—and perhaps more effectiveness. Board members should continually be looking for appropriate ways to recognize the services of the faculty.

---

[13]Mark H. Ingraham, with the collaboration of Francis P. King, *The Outer Fringe: Faculty Benefits Other Than Annuities and Insurance* (Madison WI: University of Wisconsin Press, 1965) 3.

Morale is a very important concern for all trustees. There is a difference between the sin of pride and the exhilaration one feels in the pull of God's purpose and in the presence of the leadership of the Holy Spirit. The world is continually changing and challenging the presence of God, the validity of his revelation, and the hope of eternal life. The kind of world in which the Christian institution works and witnesses today demands nothing less than the highest spiritual and academic goals; otherwise, "they, measuring themselves by themselves and comparing themselves among themselves, are not wise" (2 Cor. 10:12).

Underlying all else is the spirit of the institution, says Earl McGrath. "No feature of life on a campus is more crucial in determining the total effectiveness of an institution than the spirit with which the members of the academic community go about their daily activities."[14] The trustees can contribute to this general rapport by creative communication with the president and staff, faculty, students, alumni, denominational constituency, and local community.

If approached individually with adverse criticism, trustees should act—not overreact. They should be courteous and patient; if the complaint is substantive, they should ask for charges in writing, with supportive evidence; they should communicate immediately with the administration; and they should avoid precipitate statements to the press, since individuals should not speak for the board unless they are authorized, and since all sides should be heard before a decision is rendered. A part of the trust obligation for the whole board is to investigate charges and to take prompt action if they are found to be true. However, the more usual and positive role of trustees toward the constituency and the general public is to assert the institution's faithful adherence to its statement of purpose, to express confidence in the administration and faculty, and to point out the quality of service being rendered by the graduates.

In 1982, president W. Randall Lolley of Southeastern Baptist Theological Seminary, in his introduction to the *Trustee Manual* for that institution, wrote of esprit de corps as "the most critical quality in enabling us to fulfill our purpose. We are indeed 'out in the weather together' doing a

[14]McGrath, *Study,* 40.

THE TRUSTEE   [117]

significant job, and when the trustees come to campus we like to think that reinforcements have arrived." One of the most important, though intangible, contributions that trustees can make is to instill in all the institutional family such understanding, commitment, and pride that the morale of all is strengthened and maintained at a high level. The total effort of a board of trustees of a Christian institution should be directed toward this sense of Christian community.

This chapter is a composite of the author's speeches on trusteeship and the following works published by him on this subject:

Duties and Responsibilities of College and University Trustees, Special Report 3-69 (Raleigh NC: North Carolina Board of Higher Education, 1969).

"Duties and Responsibilities of Trustees," chapter 5 in *Planning for Higher Education in North Carolina,* Special Report 2-68 (Raleigh NC: North Carolina Board of Higher Education, 1968).

An Orientation Manual for Trustees of Church-Related Colleges, 4th ed., rev. (Nashville TN: Education Commission of the Southern Baptist Convention, 1980).

Orientation Manual for the Trustees of North Carolina Baptist Colleges, Universities, and Social Service Institutions (Raleigh NC: Baptist State Convention of North Carolina, 1981).

Trustee Handbook (Buies Creek NC: Campbell University, 1984).

Trustee Manual: An Orientation Manual for the Trustees of Southeastern Baptist Theological Seminary, Lilly Endowment project (Wake Forest NC: Southeastern Baptist Theological Seminary, 1981).

Permission has been granted by all publishers above to use the author's words in this chapter without sentence-by-sentence footnotes.

CHAPTER 13

The Teacher

The possession of the faith is . . . the proper qualification of the professor
who would wish to communicate a critical understanding of it.

—JOHN COURTNEY MURRAY, S.J.

The determining factor in the nature and effectiveness of a Christian
university is the faith and commitment of the teacher. To agree on the
theological presuppositions of the university, to establish the educational
goals, and to adopt the statement of aims and objectives all mean little or
nothing apart from the Christian self-understanding of the teacher. This
religious commitment is what distinguishes Christian teachers from their
colleagues in secular education. While faith is the motivating force, faith
without competence is dead. Competence without concern for the student
is contradictory, and competence in the discipline without the ability to
use subject matter to transmit Christian values is sterile.

In his book *The Christian Teacher* Perry D. LeFevre has pointed out
that the mission of the Christian teacher can best be defined and understood in the context of all Christian vocation. "The Christian vocation in
the larger sense, the living of a Christian life, takes its meaning from the
concrete situation in which we find ourselves as men and women." A large
part of the human situation, LeFevre says, can be talked about in words of
wonder, joy, and gratitude, but

if these factors in man's life represented the whole of his existence, religions of salvation and redemption like the Christian faith would be ir-

relevant. We might still celebrate man's dependence on God the Creator, but the whole redemptive thrust of God's historical activity in Jesus Christ would be uncalled for, meaningless. It is because the human situation is also a predicament, because evil is mixed with the good in human life, that the message of Jesus Christ is a gospel, a good news, for it is the message of the redemption of man.[1]

The teacher, in every sense, is a bearer of this good news, and thus good teachers transmit not only the subject matter of their disciplines but their own Christian experience. Such acts do not pose either a threat of indoctrination or a compromise to the integrity of their discipline. Teachers' sense of Christian vocation means that their faith and their teaching cannot be separated.

One of the notable clichés that turns up again and again in the literature of church-related colleges is the idea that church-related education is an education with a "plus," as if the plus were a mere decorative topping. The good news that the teacher transmits because of a sense of vocation is not a footnote or an afterthought or window-dressing or something tacked on. It arises out of the Christian implications and applications of the subject matter.

LeFevre has also pointed out in an especially effective way that the Christian teacher's motivation should always be grounded in Christ.

> The Christian's understanding of himself and his world as well as his motivation is grounded in Christ. In whatever way such grounding takes place, and there are many ways, the reference point for meaning is his own experience of Christ. It is this, with all that it implies, that differentiates the Christian from the non-Christian. The first Christians came to their understanding of the world and of God through Christ. They came to a new relationship to the world and to God through Christ. In the midst of all the threats to man's life, in the face of the tragic character of human existence, they came to understand and feel the power for salvation, for fulfillment, and for the transmutation if not the abo-

---

[1] Perry D. LeFevre, *The Christian Teacher* (New York: Abingdon Press, 1958) 14-15.

lition of tragedy through their encounter with Christ. They found themselves in the hands of a power not their own, of an otherness which spoke to them in their situation, which grasped them and drew them beyond themselves, remaking them in its own image and likeness, empowering them for their life in the world. Something of this initiating experience, whatever forms it may take and whatever interpretations may be given to it, informs the life, the vocation, and the work of the committed Christian teacher. The meaning of the Christian teacher's vocation is framed within a differing stream of experience. His self-understanding finds its illumination in Christ.[2]

When Myron Wicke, in his book *On Teaching in a Christian College,* lists some of the characteristics of a competent teacher, he points out that one of the prime requirements is "abilities and understanding in a broad area. Teachers must, therefore, be liberally trained. They must continue to expand the area of their understanding."[3] Piety and faith must never be a substitute for command of subject matter, or the student will be deprived. Of all persons, Christian teachers must strive for not only competence in their own field but even a more difficult goal of becoming motivating communicators. Their students must be encouraged not only to acquire knowledge but to understand how knowledge is related to their personal goals and to the world in which they live.

Moreover, as Robert Sandin has pointed out in *The Search for Excellence,* contemplation without commitment is unproductive.

Sceptical indecision threatens to cut the heart out of instruction in American schools. It is being forgotten that education must aim at a responsible and judicious choice between alternatives. A mature scholar knows what to believe, and he also knows when doubt is justified; but he cannot act as though all opinions were equally credible or equally

---

[2]Ibid., 25-26.

[3]Myron F. Wicke, *On Teaching in a Christian College,* Studies in Christian Higher Education, No. 6 (Nashville TN: Division of Higher Education, Board of Education, Methodist Church, 1961) 14-15.

dubitable. Education ought to lead not to a sophomoric relativism, but to the firming up of convictions and the settling of opinions.[4]

Faith and competence are two great requirements for the Christian teacher, but faith and competence, unless they find expression in a deep love and concern for students, have no meaning and little application. The vocation of the Christian teacher is a call to help the student deal with the concrete realities of a harsh world. It is a call to deal with the plague of pessimism. It is a call to confront barren existential philosophies, which rob human beings of any religious dimension. It is a call for the restoration of integrity and responsible citizenship. It is a call to revive in students a sense of personal purpose. It is a call to passionate and militant action against injustice and prejudice wherever they are found. It is a call to have the heart and mind of Christ, who fed the hungry, healed the sick, comforted the dying, and ministered to the smallest needs of men and women—even to a cup of water. It is a call to transmit Christian values and ethics; and above all it is a call to deal with the contemporary.

Given the current state of society, a major goal of the Christian university in today's world should be not only to help students deal with their personal problems but to send them into the world with a determination to help those who need help. Too many times students are no better equipped to deal with the problems of existence when they graduate than they were when they entered college. This youth-oriented society has made almost a fetish of shielding the young. No one likes to teach or talk about the ugly, the unpleasant, the terrifying, and the bewildering; but all persons, regardless of condition or background, sooner or later face many of life's harsher realities: illness, death, unemployment, divorce, disappointment, and injustice. A compelling reason for reappraisal of the effectiveness of a strong program in liberal arts education is the need to assist students to respond to the realities of life and to relate what they learn to the way they live. A Christian university may be very proficient in transmitting knowledge, but unless its teachers have enabled its graduates to cope with life and to assist others to cope, it has failed in its mission.

---

[4]Robert T. Sandin, *The Search for Excellence: The Christian College in an Age of Educational Competition* (Macon GA: Mercer University Press, 1982) 126-27.

The fear of indoctrinating and the problem of distinguishing between the objective and the subjective have kept many teachers—even if they are committed Christians, competent in their field and concerned about their students—from taking one of the most decisive and difficult steps of all, that of communicating the Christian values that arise naturally out of their own academic disciplines.

In certain problem areas the need for reconciliation with Christian values and with the Christian view of reality is particularly urgent. One of these areas is sociology. As children of the Enlightenment, many sociologists developed a firm belief in the scientific method, rejected revelation, showed a general distrust in theology, and later had a close affinity with positivism. However, some now maintain that sociology is outgrowing its positivistic evaluation of religion and is more ready to accept faith as a given factor in human behavior, if only in the realm of "private consciousness." James W. Jones, writing in a 1982 issue of *Cross Currents,* talks of "social theorists who charted the course of modernity" and asserts that they

> were not indifferent to the plight of religion . . . [which] is banished from the public domain and simultaneously makes itself at home in the private sphere. Thrown from the center of the collective conscience by our growing preoccupation with new possibilities of understanding the universe, controlling nature, and restructuring the social order, religion lodges in the recesses of private consciousness.[5]

Its relegation to the private domain Jones calls secularization, and he admits that this process deprives religion of its social legitimacy and confines it to "the domain of subjectivity."

This is precisely the kind of confinement that Christianity by its very nature cannot tolerate. Christian faith never has its full meaning, as has been pointed out, apart from community. A private religion that does not well up and spill over into meaningful social relations is pure mysticism. Jesus worked with his hands, walked the dusty roads, had fellowship with sinners, and in the parable of the Good Samaritan gave his followers a def-

---

[5]James W. Jones, "The Delicate Dialectic: Religion and Psychology in the Modern World," *Cross Currents* 32:2 (Summer 1982): 49.

inition of *neighbor*. To be Christian is to be involved redemptively in the human situation.

Besides sociology, several other equally challenging problem areas could be enumerated, such as psychology, psychoanalysis, history, and the natural sciences; but ultimately all teachers must examine their own fields and, if they are to do their best as Christian educators, find the best ways to transmit through their disciplines Christian values as well as cultural ones.

The whole question of the teacher's responsibility for transmitting values has become a critical issue in general education. Many individual teachers in both private and public universities have renounced responsibility for anything except the transmission of knowledge. Moral or ethical education, they claim, is so subjective that it is a matter of private and personal opinion only.

The growing public reaction is to be noted in the increasing demand for moral education that deals effectively with honesty, truthfulness, good citizenship, respect for the rights of others, courtesy, kindness, and ordinary decency. In several large urban public school systems, McGuffey's Readers have been reintroduced for two main reasons: moral teachings and basic soundness of method. Thousands of copies of these nineteenth-century textbooks have already been distributed, and perhaps the most amazing finding is their immense popularity with pupils as well as parents.

Many times today in a Christian university one hears repeated the old cliché "Values are caught and not taught." Not only is this statement suspect, but one wonders whether it is not sometimes used by the teacher as an excuse not to perform one of the most difficult of all duties, that of identifying and transmitting values as well as knowledge.

Interestingly enough, this question is one of the most ancient of educational problems. In the Platonic dialogue carried on by Meno, Socrates, and Anytus (a slave of Meno), the following question is propounded: "Can you tell me, Socrates, whether virtue is acquired by teaching or by practice; or if neither by teaching nor practice, then whether it comes to man by nature, or in what other way?" Socrates' ultimate answer is that virtue in the sense that it can be identified as knowledge can be taught, and that the value of this teaching is to help the student form right opinions. On the other hand, Socrates views virtue as a gift of God. "Then, Meno, the conclusion is that virtue comes to the virtuous by the gift of God, but we shall never know the certain truth until, before asking how virtue is given, we inquire into the actual nature of virtue."[6] This inquiry into the nature of virtue becomes the subject matter of moral education, varying from one discipline to another.

To ask whether values are caught *or* taught is to put the question falsely, implying that there is only one of two ways that values can be communicated. The truth is that, in the formation of character, better results come from the character of the teacher than from any specific knowledge that he or she might transmit. If teachers never bring up the subject of values in their classrooms, however, any effect that their influence might have is considerably lessened.

This assertion brings up the whole matter of the character of teachers themselves. Admittedly one of the most complex and hazardous tasks an administrator ever undertakes is selecting teachers, setting up criteria by which to evaluate them and passing judgment on their qualifications. In at least one university the attempt to consider "qualities such as 'character,' 'leadership,' 'personality,' and 'cooperation'" has been ruled out because a distinguished committee made the categorical statement as early as 1939 that "such qualities are extremely difficult to assess" and that "there is a certain danger . . . in giving them emphasis."[7] This committee concluded that "personal characteristics should not be considered as primary criteria," and their conclusion was reported in 1982 by the president of their university. "In this fashion, the earlier emphasis on character was pushed aside, save in exceptional cases, as incompatible with the standards of academic freedom and scholarly excellence that seemed more and more essential to the modern university."[8]

---

[6]"Meno," in Plato, *The Dialogues*, 174, 190.

[7]From *Report on Some Problems of Personnel in the Faculty of Arts and Sciences* (Cambridge: Harvard University Press, 1939) 77, quoted by Derek Bok in *Beyond the Ivory Tower*, 118.

[8]Bok, *Beyond the Ivory Tower*, 119.

Leaving aside the question of the character of the teacher and focusing on the matter of the character of the education he or she imparts, one finds a general default in this area in both public and private institutions of higher learning. Such a default offers the Christian university in today's world an opportunity so valuable that it dares not fail to seize the initiative. Nowhere is the general attitude toward moral education better demonstrated than in the book just quoted, Derek Bok's *Beyond the Ivory Tower: Social Responsibilities of the Modern University.*

Three of Bok's statements are of singular interest: (1) that character has become a concept so subjective and relative that it no longer can be used as a major criterion for the employment and promotion of faculty; (2) that the conduct of students or faculty on or off the campus, as long as it does not interfere with the essential workings of the university, is solely a matter for civil authorities; and (3) that if a scholar is "the best available . . . to teach and write in a given field," the university should not be deprived of his or her services.[9]

An inconsistency should be pointed out. At the same time that the term *character* is rejected as being too subjective, *competence* is reaffirmed as the major criterion for both employment and retention of faculty. While some external, objective standards can undoubtedly be set up for judging competence, this is in many ways as elusive and subjective a term as *character.* One would find it difficult to justify a decision on competence by offering objective evidence alone.

A more rational view for the Christian university would hold that there are sufficient objective criteria to make reasonable value judgments concerning both character and competence but that there is always a risk of error because of the complex human factors involved. The basic problem is not methodology but philosophy, and willingness to consider the subjective qualifications of the good teacher.

The teacher in a Christian university in today's world should above all be a harbinger of hope. Certitudes based upon an uncritical faith in the power of education, the power of scientific research, and the power of technology to open new vistas to enlightened individuals and to solve society's

[9]Ibid., 119, 31.

most pressing problems have all but collapsed. People foresee a day when they may be cowering in the ruins of their own Tower of Babel, which they constructed with such hope and joy.

Pessimism concerning man's future, people's inability to find an authentic way of life, their cynicism, and their loss of faith is reflected in the growing anxiety of modern man. "The Christian answer is that we have God's assurances in Christ that every life has infinite value, eternal purpose, and eternal meaning. This is the truth of the resurrection: not release from inevitable tragedies, suffering, and pain of human existence; not eternal death after a meaningless life; but eternal life for those who claim the promises of God in Christ."[10] This is the antidote for the pestilence of pessimism. The authentic life is in the knowledge that we may be sick, yet well; dying, yet living; weak, yet strong; foolish, yet wise; troubled, yet at peace; blind, yet seeing; stumbling, yet not falling; with diminishing powers, yet with undiminished hope. To this knowledge the Christian teacher can testify, and also to the truth that those burdens that God does not lift, he gives his children the strength to bear.

---

[10]Ben C. Fisher, "What Must Modern Man Do to Be Saved?" *Southern Baptist Educator* 42:6 (July-August 1978): 11.

CHAPTER 14

The Student

The only reasonable way to judge a college is not by the size of its campus or by the abundance of its financial resources or by the number of books in its library or even by the publications of its professors. The college is to be judged by the quality of its human product.

—ELTON TRUEBLOOD

When scholars a generation or two from now review the many excellent and thoughtful papers that have been written about higher education in the last fifty years, one of the questions they may ask is, Why was so little said about the student as a person? The publications in question are replete with remedies for deficiency in educational philosophy, academic freedom, course offerings, value identification, teacher preparation, facilities and equipment, library accessions, collective bargaining, interinstitutional cooperation, accreditation standards, community service, industrial and business relations, trustee orientation, and university governance. In a surprisingly large proportion of these studies, the student is never mentioned, directly or indirectly, even though the authors would say with conviction that the institutions they represent exist solely for the good of the student.

Failure to understand this absence of reference to the student will make it very difficult to appreciate the nature of the student revolt of the 1950s and 1960s. Their revolution focused on many legitimate educational and political issues, but it derived its passionate impetus from the students' perception of the absence of feeling, from emotional malnutrition. There is a piece of folk music sung by Conway Twitty and climaxed with an insight that speaks poignantly to students' resentment about their place as categories, not persons, in the priorities of the university: "You love the circus, but you don't love the clown." Joan Baez expressed it another way in one of her ballads that was a favorite with students: "You are the orphans in the land of no tomorrows."

Most references to students in books on education are oblique, secondary, or statistical. Students are almost totally the object. In these times the wealthy, prestigious universities have sought special categories of students whose abilities are calculated to enhance the universities' reputation. The less prestigious schools have sought students to fill classrooms, balance budgets, and even to achieve survival. There is nothing wrong with wanting either high academic standards or survival as an educational institution, but compassion for the student as person and the major concerns just mentioned are not mutually exclusive. There is a serious imbalance here that the Christian university particularly should seek to correct.

However, the Christian institution of higher learning can no longer simply express in idealistic terms what it intends to do for students in preparing them vocationally, developing them aesthetically, and providing the context in which they can choose personal values and lasting life goals. University personnel should ask three questions: (1) Do we have adequate understanding of today's college student? (2) Do we understand the enormous changes that have taken place in almost every aspect of the social order? (3) What indications are there that the university has personal and intelligent concern about the student?

There is much evidence that American colleges and universities, public and private, are not fully aware of the differing problems, pressures, and preparation of today's entering freshman. Assumptions that were held to be axiomatic twenty-five years ago are being called into question. For example, John Naisbitt in his book *Megatrends* declares that "the generation graduating from high school today is the first generation in American history to graduate less skilled than its parents." Naisbitt bases this observation in part on the Carnegie Council Policy Studies in Higher Education, which stated that "because of deficits in our public school system, about one-third of our youth are ill-educated, ill-employed, and ill-equipped to make their way in American society."[1]

Even as late as a decade ago, American educators were speaking with pride about the enormous strides American secondary education had made in teacher training, curriculum development, superior equipment, and more adequate physical plants. Moreover, educators assumed that mass communication media had made students world citizens, aware of revolutionary social, economic, and cultural changes. It was also evident that students had access to unlimited types of information. Furthermore, because of the large amount of leisure time unknown to previous generations, it was believed that they had more time to think, to learn, to experiment, and to participate in a wide range of social and cultural activities.

Because of these advantages, it was assumed that students entering college in the 1950s and 1960s were the best prepared and most mature ever to enter the American university system. They undoubtedly had the ability to ask probing questions about religion, sex, morals, politics, customs, manners, and so forth. They also were observed to have the knack for detecting sham and the courage to speak up—to the dismay of both parents and teachers. But more important, students began to assert their individualism and became rebellious toward family and toward all types of institutional control.

The radical student revolt of the fifties and sixties has forced a reconsideration, especially about the maturity of the student. Most students were certainly better informed than any previous generation, but in retrospect they were precocious rather than mature. Freedom gave way to license, radical individualism degenerated into violence, and the rejection of values left many students alienated from society—even to the point of suicide. Nevertheless, there is overwhelming evidence that colleges and universities were caught almost completely by surprise because they had lived in a world apart and because many faculty members apparently were totally unaware of the impending crisis and the radically altered social matrix.

---

[1]John Naisbitt, *Megatrends: Ten New Directions Transforming Our Lives* (New York: Warner Books, 1982) 31-32.

Student revolutions were massive and often contradictory. Demonstrations for peace frequently wound up in rioting and serious destruction of property. The radical New Left included the Student Non-Violent Coordinating Committee, but under Stokely Carmichael nonviolence gave way to violence and laid the groundwork for the Black Power Movement and later the Black Panthers. In the end the Students for Democratic Society fared little better, and even though it was perhaps the most influential of the student organizations, it eventually fragmented, also forsaking earlier nonviolent vows. It should be noted that the Weathermen, who were the most radically violent of these groups, for the most part came from middle-class and upper-middle-class backgrounds.

Far too little attention has been given to analysis of the pressures and changes in almost every aspect of human existence that produced this student revolt. What is evident is that, following World War II, students were under demands that had not previously existed. The issues of war and peace, nuclear holocaust, environmental deterioration, social injustice, and world hunger were taken far more seriously by young people than their parents or teachers supposed. Watching on national television women and children being burned alive by napalm and viewing movies such as *On the Beach* produced in many students not only fear but cynicism, anger, and distrust for constituted authority.

Their immaturity was evidenced, however, in the course that their cynicism and anger and distrust took. In spite of all their protesting about concern for the individual, they were cause oriented rather than person oriented. Toward those disagreeing they used invective, abuse, and violence instead of reason. While protesting for freedom they violated the freedom of any who took exception to their views, frequently shouting opponents down or threatening them with bodily harm. Students volunteered idealistically for causes, but in many instances turned off their loyalties as suddenly as they had turned them on. One of the sadder aspects of this episode was the absence of constructive ideas. For the most part, students vented their outrage indiscriminately against parents, teachers, and institutions without troubling themselves to determine who was actually to blame or what was a practical remedy.

To be sure, many were motivated by idealism, but some indeed were bored and looking for excitement; and because they had sufficient private financial resources, they were able to indulge their fancies without ever once having run any great risk or made any real sacrifice. Among the first to observe this hypocrisy were the blacks, for whom *white liberalism* became a dirty term.

In retrospect, most knowledgeable observers agree that the more violent events of the student revolt would never have taken place had it not been for the active involvement of radical young faculty members, some acting openly and some covertly. As Sidney Hook pointed out, "The faint of heart among their teachers turn on their own principled colleagues and administrative leaders. These militants succeed in sowing distrust among students who do not see through their strategy. They also succeed in dividing the faculties."[2] This situation, along with the inertia and complete noninvolvement of most of the rest of the faculty, created the conditions that came close to wrecking American higher education.

In 1971, the Carnegie Commission produced a comprehensive study entitled *Dissent and Disruption: Proposals for Consideration by the Campus.* This research exercised considerable influence in restructuring college and university governance. The report views the problem of dissent and disruption primarily in terms of structural deficiencies and the absence of consistent procedural processes. This sound approach probably was one of the reasons for eventually restoring order.

However, the weakness of the report is that it did not penetrate the basic problem but treated symptoms only. Consider an example of its analysis.

Had the machinery of university decision-making been in better order, the students' demands and actions could have been dealt with without convulsions. And as long as the machinery for decisions on university-wide issues remains as it is in most American universities, such issues will arise. If the rate of increase in financial support declines, these issues will precipitate rancour within the teaching and research staffs of the universities.[3]

---

[2]"The Long View," in Sidney Hook, ed., *In Defense of Academic Freedom* (New York: Pegasus, 1971) 18.

[3]Edward Shils: "The Hole in the Centre: University Government in the United

Unfortunately there is little evidence to show that faculty, administration, or trustees in the 1950s and 1960s would have paid much heed to
basic student demands for participation in governance, even if the machinery later recommended had then been in place. Not only was concern lacking, but apparently in spite of all the talk about commitment to academic
freedom and democracy, there was both neglect and abuse of both—and
sometimes downright arbitrariness. The result was that during the revolt
many faculty members and administrators made "startling concessions . . .
in an atmosphere marked by physical threat, fear, and guilt."[4] Driven by
this fear and guilt and by the belated recognition of the justice of many of
the student demands, faculty action in some cases came close to surrender-
ing all authority, particularly in such sensitive areas as responsibility for
student conduct—either on or off the campus. None were more jubilant in
announcing the demise of the principle of in loco parentis than the faculty.
Along with "outmoded petty rules," however, personal concern for the
student was all but abandoned.

Because of the relative quiet on the educational front today and the
seeming docility of students, who are now much more preoccupied with
finding jobs and choosing vocations that are likely to guarantee employment, many observers are beguiled into thinking that the radicalism of the
sixties is over. This is a dangerous assumption; as James A. Michener said
in his book *Kent State*, "This could be your university. The students and
National Guardsmen could be you, or young people of your neighborhood,
or, if you are old enough, your sons and daughters. The city of Kent could
be your community. That is why you need to know what happened to you,
so that you can prevent it from happening again."[5]

States," *Minerva*, January 1970, quoted in *Dissent and Disruption: Proposals for Consideration by the Campus*, Report and Recommendations by the Carnegie Commission on Higher Education (New York: McGraw-Hill, 1971) 66.

[4]Phyllis Keller, *Getting at the Core: Curricular Reform at Harvard* (Cambridge:
Harvard University Press, 1982) 32.

[5]James A. Michener, *Kent State: What Happened and Why* (New York: Random House, 1971) foreword.

The student revolution of the 1950s and 1960s did have its positive aspects and raised an effective voice for much-needed educational reform, particularly in curriculum, classroom teaching, governance, and social concern. Nevertheless, the Christian university in today's world is confronted with a new crisis, different but no less severe, produced by a growing secular culture, in which the Christian view of the family, ethics, moral responsibility, and values is less and less influential. The question must be raised: Are faculties today any more aware of this challenge than were the good dons of the fifties and sixties aware of theirs?

While many would like to think that the majority of college students do not use drugs, belong to no radical new movements, are not sexually promiscuous, harbor no ill feelings against their parents, do not lie or cheat or steal, do not drink, and do not respond to the appeals of far-out religious cults and subcultures, evidence indicates that at best these are open questions, however unpleasant the answers may prove to be. The troubling statistics continue to pour in about the ever-increasing use of alcohol and drugs in high school and even in grade school. The number of teenage unmarried mothers continues to rise, and there is less and less stigma attached to living together out of wedlock. There is also growing evidence that in high school, particularly, cheating has become almost a way of life, so that there is no particular blame attached to it. Shoplifting is too often a game, as much so for some of the affluent as for the poor. Even the youngest teenage girl, if she tries to follow traditional values, runs the risk of being labeled "out of it."

These are some of the more visible and damaging pressures to which all students are subjected, and these peer pressures and societal forces affect student response to any Christian teachings about the family, citizenship, and participation in the life of the church. Today's Christian university must take into account the fact that society is no longer on its side.

Yet, the academic community itself seems to have too shallow an understanding of the present generation of college students. For the past several years, an almost endless procession of speakers and writers have addressed their college audiences with the questions, Who am I? Where am I going?—as if every student were struggling with an identity problem and deeply concerned about social issues. The truth of the matter is that what universities are dealing with today is ultimately far more dangerous than radical revolt and degenerate life-styles. Many students are not asking profound questions. They have no deep yearnings, and they tend to ride with—not swim against—any strong current in which they find themselves trapped. Or like sheep, they browse contentedly on either stubble or lush grass in the vast valley of inertia.

Any university—Christian or otherwise—in today's world is now confronted with students who have been brought up in a world where more change has taken place within the last hundred years than since the dawn of recorded history. The Industrial Revolution, two world wars, the development of mass communication media, mobility, and technology have been external forces that have radically reordered society.

The innate goodness of man—the concept of the "noble savage" who possessed within his genes inborn capacities for goodness and boundless progress—somehow has not been demonstrated. The flaw in this theory was the half-truth discussed in an earlier chapter, for man inherently has the capacity for evil as well as good, as the Judeo-Christian tradition has always maintained. The system of education that grew out of the "noble savage" idea stressed the uninhibited development of personality to the neglect of knowledge and values; and it has been demonstrated in a number of recent studies that, on the level of knowledge alone, a shocking number of well-adjusted, socially integrated students have graduated from high school without the ability to read, write, do simple arithmetic, or identify geographic locations. As a result, within this culture there has been a leveling off of the knowledge one could assume to be basic. Traditional norms have been replaced, to a large degree, by relativism—if they have not been obliterated entirely. Charles Eliot's noble elective system has in the main failed for three reasons: overoptimism about the capacity of even the best qualified and most carefully selected student to determine what his or her curriculum should be; the breakdown in liberal arts education in favor of megaversity, where specialization takes place too narrowly and too early; and the failure in general preparatory education to furnish basic knowledge.

Moreover, secular education's preoccupation with the objective has virtually eliminated any serious attempt to transmit religious or even cultural values. This deficiency has had a very profound and negative effect on citizenship, the understanding and application of justice, and the quality of leadership in present-day society. One can appeal to history for the ultimate results of a society that no longer inculcates either religious or humane values. The same countries that gave the world the Universities of Bologna and Padua, Heidelberg, Tübingen, and Marburg also produced the intellectual community's capitulation to and cooperation with Mussolini and Hitler. Sister Alice Gallin describes the shock of this realization.

> One bitterly cold afternoon in January 1972 I found myself interviewing Albert Speer in the living room of his charming family home in Heidelberg. There below us was the picturesque medieval university which has been the subject of so much romantic song and story. The paradox struck me forcibly: that a man could grow up and be educated in a country with the intellectual tradition of Germany and end up in jail for twenty years because of his complicity in the crimes against humanity of the Nazi Brownshirts. As he explained to me his failure to ask questions ". . . because [he] did not want to know the answers" when he visited the work camps of the Third Reich, my mind tried to come to terms with the inner contradictions. The humanization which is assumed to be the goal of education had not even enabled men to recognize the dehumanization of the crimes revealed at Nuremberg? What then can be the relationship between learning and life, between academics and politics?[6]

One of the amazing findings of the Feldman-Newcomb study, *The Impact of College on Students,* is that faculty members are not responsible for any significant changes that take place in students. It is to be hoped that this statement is much less true of Christian colleges and universities than of higher education generally, but it cannot be ignored. The Christian college or university is dedicated to the belief that, if teachers understand their students, as well as the societal forces that impinge upon them, and *if teach-*

---

[6]Alice Gallin, "Academia and Politics: The German Experience, 1925-33" manuscript, 1. This manuscript has now been revised and published as *Midwives to Nazism: University Professors in Weimar Germany, 1925-1933* (Macon GA: Mercer University Press, 1986). See especially the introduction and conclusion of the book.

ers exercise for their students as persons the same concern that Christian parents do for their children, then only will idealized statements of purpose concerning values, life goals, and responsible citizenship become living reality and not merely sounding brass and a tinkling cymbal.

Jacques Barzun in his oft-quoted *Teacher in America* has made two pertinent observations. There are teachers who are remembered "for inspiring, guiding, and teaching decisively at a critical time." And "The whole aim of good teaching is to turn the young learner, by nature a little copycat, into an independent, self-propelling creature, who can not merely learn but study— that is, work as his own boss to the limit of his powers. This is to turn pupils into students."[7]

In light of these insights, the challenge to the Christian university in today's world becomes fourfold:

1. To deal more adequately and seriously with those exceptional students who are asking the right questions.

2. To guide those students who are asking the wrong questions— or the right questions for the wrong reasons.

3. Possibly the greatest challenge of all: To stimulate those students who ask no questions, expect no answers, and are contented forever to drift with the currents.

4. To present the Christian view of man.

---

[7]Jacques Barzun, *Teacher in America* (Boston: Little, Brown, 1945) 21.

OTHER REFERENCES

Avorn, Jerry L., and members of the staff of the *Columbia Daily Spectator*. *Up against the Ivy Wall: A History of the Columbia Crisis*. New York: Atheneum, 1968.

Feldman, Kenneth A., and Theodore M. Newcomb. *The Impact of College on Students*. Vol. 1. San Francisco: Jossey-Bass Publishers, 1970.

Sanford, Nevitt, ed. *College and Character*. A briefer version of *The American College*. New York: John Wiley & Sons, 1964.

Strommen, Merton P., Milo L. Brekke, Ralph C. Underwager, and Arthur L. Johnson. *A Study of Generations*. Minneapolis: Augsburg Publishing House, 1972.

Bibliography

Widely ranging references are included here: recent studies, classics, and works that attempt to set higher education in its social and cultural context. Within the religious category, there are statements from many different denominations, all wrestling with essentially the same problems.

AAUP Policy Documents and Reports. Washington, D.C.: American Association of University Professors, 1977.

Abraham, Henry J. *Freedom and the Court: Civil Rights and Liberties in the United States*. New York: Oxford University Press, 1972.

Achieving the Mission of Church-Related Institutions of Liberal Learning. Proceedings of Dialogue at Rockhurst College, Kansas City MO, 29-30 November 1976. Washington, D.C.: Association of American Colleges, 1977.

"Ad Interim Committee on Higher Education, Report and Recommendations." *Minutes of the 117th General Assembly of the Presbyterian Church in the United States*, pt. 1, pp. 207-208, 214. Atlanta: Stated Clerk of the General Assembly, 1977.

Agar, Herbert. *The Price of Union*. Boston: Houghton Mifflin, 1950.

Altizer, Thomas J. J., and William Hamilton. *Radical Theology and the Death of God*. Indianapolis IN: Bobbs-Merrill, 1966.

American Association of University Professors, American Council on Education, and Association of Governing Boards of Universities and Colleges. *Statement on Government of Colleges and Universities*. Reprinted from *AAUP Bulletin 52* (Winter 1966). Washington, D.C.: American Association of University Professors, n.d.

Aristotle. *Nicomachean Ethics*. Vol. 9 of *Great Books of the Western World*. Chicago: Encyclopedia Britannica, 1952.

Association of American Colleges. *The Contribution of the Church-Related Higher Education*. Minneapolis: Augsburg Publishing House, 1977.

Astin, Alexander W. *Four Critical Years: Effects of College on Beliefs, Attitudes, and Knowledge*. San Francisco: Jossey-Bass Publishers, 1978.

Athearn, Walter S. *Religious Education in American Democracy*. Boston: Pilgrim Press, 1917.

Augustine. *The City of God*. Translated by John Healey and edited by R. V. G. Tasker. Everyman's Library, No. 982. London: J. M. Dent & Sons, 1950.

Averill, Lloyd J. *The Church College and the Public Good*. Washington, D.C.: Council of Protestant Colleges and Universities, 1969.

_____. *A Strategy for the Protestant College*. Philadelphia: Westminster Press, 1966.

Avorn, Jerry L., and members of the staff of the *Columbia Daily Spectator*. *Up against the Ivy Wall: A History of the Columbia Crisis*. New York: Atheneum, 1968.

Axelrad, Albert S. "Religious Faith and Higher Education: A View from a Jewish-Sponsored University." *NICM Journal* 2 (Fall 1977): 60-71.

Ayer, A. J., ed. *Logical Positivism*. New York: Macmillan, Free Press, 1959.

Baepler, Richard, William H. K. Narum, Arthur L. Olsen, Myles Stenshoel, and Nelvin Vos. *The Quest for a Viable Saga: The Church-Related College in an Age of Pluralism*. Valparaiso IN: Association of Lutheran College Faculties, 1977.

Bailyn, Bernard. *Education in the Forming of American Society*. Chapel Hill NC: University of North Carolina Press, 1960.

Bainton, Roland Herbert. *The Travail of Religious Liberty*. Philadelphia: Westminster Press, 1951.

Baptist Education Study Task. Summations of Twenty-Four Regional Seminars, Two National Study Conferences, and the Report of the Findings Committee, 2d ed., rev. Nashville TN: Education Commission of the Southern Baptist Convention, 1978.

Baptist Joint Committee on Public Affairs Staff Report. *Two Supreme Court Decisions*. Washington, D.C.: Baptist Joint Committee on Public Affairs, 1968.

Baptists and Reformed in Dialogue. Studies from the World Alliance of Reformed Churches. Geneva: World Alliance of Reformed Churches, 1984.

Barbour, Ian G. *Science and Secularity*. New York: Harper & Row, Publishers, 1970.

Barnette, Henlee H. *The Drug Crisis and the Church*. Philadelphia: Westminster Press, 1971.

Barzun, Jacques. *Teacher in America*. Boston: Little, Brown, 1945.

Baum, Gregory. *Man Becoming: God in Secular Experience*. New York: Seabury Press, 1970.

Beach, Waldo. *Conscience on Campus: An Interpretation of Christian Ethics for College Life*. New York: Association Press, Haddam House Book, 1958.

Bell, Daniel. *The Reforming of General Education*. New York: Columbia University Press, 1966.

Bell, Sadie. *The Church, the State, and Education in Virginia*. New York: Arno Press, 1969.

Bell, Sister D. "A New Era in Catholic Tertiary Education." *Way Supplement* 26 (Winter 1975): 37-48.

Bender, Richard N., ed. *The Church-Related College Today: Anachronism or Opportunity?* Symposium of Papers produced by the Council on the Church-Related College. Nashville TN: General Board of Education, United Methodist Church, 1971.

Benson, Peter L., and Dorothy L. Williams. *Religion on Capitol Hill: Myths and Realities*. New York: Harper & Row, 1984.

Berdyaev, Nicolas. *The Fate of Man in the Modern World*. Ann Arbor MI: University of Michigan Press, 1935. Reprint, Ann Arbor Paperback, 1961.

Berger, Peter L. *A Rumor of Angels*. Garden City NY: Doubleday, 1970.

Berkeley, George. *The Principles of Human Knowledge*. Vol. 35 of *Great Books of the Western World*, Chicago: Encyclopedia Britannica, 1952.

Blamires, Harry. *The Christian Mind*. London: SPCK, 1963.

——————. "Implications of Christian Thought in Contemporary Culture and Education." *Southern Baptist Educator* 43 (September 1978): 3.

——————. *Where Do We Stand?* Ann Arbor MI: Servant Books, 1980.

Blau, Joseph L. *Cornerstones of Religious Freedom in America*. Boston: Beacon Press, 1950.

Bok, Derek. *Beyond the Ivory Tower: Social Responsibilities of the Modern University*. Cambridge: Harvard University Press, 1982.

Boles, Donald E. *Religion in the Public Schools.* Ames IA: State University Press, 1965.

Bolling, Landrum R. "Seedbed for Moral and Spiritual Values." *Southern Baptist Educator* 42 (January 1978): 12.

Borders, William D. "'Call to Action': Response from Catholic Colleges and Universities as Community." *Delta Epsilon Sigma Bulletin* 22 (May 1977): 40-48.

Breneman, David W., and Chester E. Finn, Jr., eds., with the assistance of Susan C. Nelson. *Public Policy and Private Higher Education: Studies in Higher Education Policy.* Washington, D.C.: Brookings Institution, 1978.

Bronowski, J. *The Ascent of Man.* Boston: Little, Brown, 1973.

Brown, Kenneth Irving. *Not Minds Alone: Some Frontiers of Christian Education.* New York: Harper & Brothers, Publishers, 1954.

Brown, Samuel Windsor. *The Secularization of American Education.* Contributions to Education, No. 49, Teachers College, Columbia University. New York: AMS Press, 1972.

Brown, William Adams, in association with a committee of American Christians appointed by the Federal Council of the Churches of Christ in America. *Church and State in Contemporary America.* New York: Scribner's Sons, 1936.

Brubacher, John S. *A History of the Problems of Education.* New York: McGraw-Hill, 1947.

―――――. *The Public Schools and Spiritual Values.* New York: Harper & Brothers, 1944.

Brubacher, John S., and Willis Rudy. *Higher Education in Transition: An American History, 1636-1956.* New York: Harper & Row, Publishers, 1958.

Buckley, William F., Jr. *God and Man at Yale: The Superstitions of Academic Freedom.* Chicago: Regnery, 1951.

Burns, Gerald P. *Trustees in Higher Education: Their Function and Coordination.* N.p.: Independent College Funds of America, 1966.

Burrell, David B., and Franzita Kane, eds. *Evangelization in the American Context.* Proceedings of a Symposium "Evangelization in the American Context: The Pastoral Presence in an Open Society," Notre Dame IN, 11-13 January 1976. Notre Dame IN: University of Notre Dame Press, 1976.

Buttrick, George A. *Biblical Thought and the Secular University.* Baton Rouge LA: Louisiana State University Press, 1960.

_____. *Christ and Man's Dilemma*. New York: Abingdon-Cokesbury Press, 1946.

_____. *Sermons Preached in a University Church*. Nashville TN: Abingdon Press, 1959.

Byron, William J. "Catholic Colleges: Why We Stay in There." *AGB* [Association of Governing Boards]*Report* 21 (May-June 1979): 27-30.

_____. "Pluralism in Higher Education." *America*, 27 July 1985.

Camus, Albert. *Resistance, Rebellion, and Death*. Translated by Justin O'Brien. New York: Knopf, 1961.

Carlson, Edgar M. *The Future of Church-Related Higher Education*. Minneapolis: Augsburg Publishing House, 1977.

Catholic Higher Education and the Pastoral Mission of the Church. Washington, D.C.: United States Catholic Conference, 1980.

"Catholic Higher Education in the 1970s." *America* 130 (26 January 1974): 45.

The Catholic University, Instrument of Cultural Pluralism to the Service of Church and Society. Thematic Report, XII General Assembly. Paris: International Federation of Catholic Universities, 1979.

"The Catholic University in the Modern World: A Statement of Position Adopted by the International Federation of Catholic Universities." *College Newsletter* 31 (December 1968): 8-9.

Chadwick, Owen. *The Secularization of the European Mind in the Nineteenth Century*. Cambridge: Cambridge University Press, 1975.

Chamberlin, J. Gordon. *Churches and the Campus*. Philadelphia: Westminster Press, 1963.

Church and College: A Vital Partnership. Vol. 1, *Affirmation;* vol. 2, *Mission;* vol. 3, *Accountability;* vol. 4, *Exchange*. Sherman TX: National Congress on Church-Related Colleges and Universities, 1980. (Published through the Center for Program and Institutional Renewal, Austin College.)

Clark, Kenneth. *Civilisation*. New York: Harper & Row, Publishers, 1969.

College Reading and Religion. Edward W. Hazen Foundation and Committee on Religion and Education of the American Council on Education. New Haven CT: Yale University Press, 1948.

Collingwood, R. G. *The Idea of History*. New York: Oxford University Press, Galaxy, 1956.

Conant, James B. *Education and Liberty: The Role of Schools in a Modern Democracy.* New York: Vintage Books, 1953.

Conrad, Clifton E., and Jean C. Wyer. *Liberal Education in Transition.* AAHE-ERIC/ Higher Education Research Report No. 3. Washington, D.C.: American Association for Higher Education, 1980.

Cornelison, Isaac A. *Relation of Religion to Civil Government in the United States of America: A State without a Church, but Not without a Religion.* Civil Liberties in American History, reprint series. New York: Da Capo Press, 1970.

Cothen, Grady C. *Faith and Higher Education.* Nashville TN: Broadman Press, 1976.

Cox, Claire. *The New-Time Religion.* Englewood Cliffs NJ: Prentice-Hall, 1961.

Cox, Harvey Gallagher. *Religion in the Secular City: Toward a Postmodern Theology.* New York: Simon & Schuster, 1984.

——————. *The Secular City.* New York: Macmillan, 1965.

"The Crisis in Higher Education: A Letter to the Churches from the NCC General Board." *Presbyterian Outlook* 150 (14 October 1968): 5-7.

Culver, Raymond B. *Horace Mann and Religion in the Massachusetts Public Schools.* American Education: Its Men, Ideas, and Institutions. New York: Arno Press and the New York Times, 1969.

Cuninggim, Merrimon. *The College Seeks Religion.* Yale Studies in Religious Education, vol. 20. New Haven CT: Yale University Press, 1947.

Cunningham, Richard B. *Christianity and Contemporary Humanism.* Louisville KY: Southern Baptist Theological Seminary, 1981.

Current Issues in Catholic Higher Education: Facing the Future 3:2 (Winter 1983).

Current Issues in Catholic Higher Education: Peace and Justice Education 1:2 (Winter 1981).

Curtis, P. "Catholic Universities Have Become More Catholic." *College Management* 5 (November 1970): 17-18.

D'Arcy, Martin C. *Humanism and Christianity.* Perspectives in Humanism, vol. 9. New York: New American Library, in association with World Publishing, 1969.

Dawson, Joseph Martin. *America's Way in Church, State, and Society.* New York: Macmillan, 1953.

Dewey, John. *A Common Faith.* New Haven CT: Yale University Press, 1934.

Dillenberger, John. *Protestant Thought and Natural Science.* Garden City NY: Doubleday, 1960.

Dissent and Disruption: Proposals for Consideration by the Campus. Report and Recommendations by the Carnegie Commission on Higher Education. New York: McGraw-Hill, 1971.

Ditmanson, Harold, and Centennial Planning Committee. *Identity and Mission in a Changing Context.* Northfield MN: St. Olaf's College, 1974.

Ditmanson, Harold H., Howard V. Hong, and Warren A. Quanbeck, eds. *Christian Faith and the Liberal Arts.* Minneapolis: Augsburg Publishing House, 1960.

Dolbeare, Kenneth M., and Phillip E. Hammond. *School Prayer Decisions: From Court Policy to Local Practice.* Chicago: University of Chicago Press, 1971.

Drushal, J. Garber. *The Church and Its Colleges: A Status Report for the United Presbyterian Church in the U.S.A.* Mission in Education, the Program Agency, United Presbyterian Church U.S.A. New York: United Presbyterian Church, U.S.A. [now Presbyterian Church (U.S.A.) with headquarters in Louisville KY], 1975.

Dugger, Ronnie. *Our Invaded Universities: Form, Reform, and New Starts.* New York: Norton, 1974.

Durant, Will, and Ariel Durant. *Story of Civilization.* Eleven vols. New York: Simon & Schuster, 1935-1975.

Durkheim, Emile. *The Elementary Forms of the Religious Life.* Translated by Joseph Ward Swain. New York: Macmillan, 1915. Reprint, Free Press, 1965.

Dutile, Fernand, and Edward McGlynn Gaffney, Jr. *State and Campus.* Notre Dame, IN: University of Notre Dame Press, 1984.

Eddington, Sir Arthur Stanley. *The Nature of the Physical World.* New York: Macmillan, 1928.

Eddy, Sherwood. *The Kingdom of God and the American Dream.* New York: Harper & Brothers, Publishers, 1941.

Eliot, T. S. *Christianity and Culture.* New York: Harcourt, Brace, 1940. Reprint, Harvest, 1949.

Endangered Service: Independent Colleges, Public Policy, and the First Amendment. Nashville TN: National Commission on United Methodist Higher Education, 1976.

Engel, David E., comp. *Religion in Public Education: Problems and Prospects.* New York: Paulist Press, 1974.

European Theology Challenged by the World-Wide Church. Report of a Consultation at Geneva, Switzerland, 29 March-2 April 1976. Occasional Paper No. 8. Geneva: Conference of European Churches, 1976.

"Expectations of Higher Education: Report on a Symposium." *Presbyterian Survey* 161 (9 July 1979): 5.

Fackre, Gabriel. *Secular Impact: The Promise of Mission.* Philadelphia: Pilgrim Press, 1968.

Faculty Development in a Time of Retrenchment. A *Change* Publication. N.p.: Group for Human Development in Higher Education and *Change* Magazine, 1974.

Fair, Charles. *The New Nonsense: The End of the Rational Consensus.* New York: Simon & Schuster, 1974.

Fairchild, Hoxie, et al. *Religious Perspectives in College Teaching.* New York: Ronald Press, 1952.

Faith and Reason in Higher Education: Vision and Tradition for the New University. Deland FL: Stetson University Centennial Publication, 1983.

Fehlig, Sister Mary Borgia. "The Emerging Role of the Catholic Two-Year Commuter College." Ph.D. diss., St. Louis University, 1968.

Feldman, Kenneth A., and Theodore M. Newcomb. *The Impact of College on Students.* Vol. 1. San Francisco: Jossey-Bass Publishers, 1970.

Ferment in Education. A Symposium at the Installation of George Dinsmore Stoddard as President of the University of Illinois. Urbana: University of Illinois Press, 1948.

Ferré, Frederick. *Shaping the Future.* New York: Harper & Row Publishers, 1976.

Ferré, Nels F. S. *Christian Faith and Higher Education.* New York: Harper & Brothers, Publishers, 1954.

Fisher, Ben C. *Duties and Responsibilities of College and University Trustees.* Special Report 3-69. Raleigh NC: North Carolina Board of Higher Education, 1969.

_____. *Orientation Manual for the Trustees of North Carolina Baptist Colleges, Universities, and Social Service Institutions.* Raleigh NC: Baptist State Convention of North Carolina, 1981.

_____. *An Orientation Manual for Trustees of Church-Related Colleges.* 4th ed., rev. Nashville TN: Education Commission of the Southern Baptist Convention, 1980.

_____. "Traveler without a Ticket." *1981-1982 Supplement to the CIC Independent* (October 1981).

_____. *Trustee Handbook.* Buies Creek NC: Campbell University, 1984.

_____. *Trustee Manual: An Orientation Manual for the Trustees of Southeastern Baptist Theological Seminary.* Lilly Endowment project. Wake Forest NC: Southeastern Baptist Theological Seminary, 1981.

_____. "What Must Modern Man Do to Be Saved?" *Southern Baptist Educator,* 42:6 (July-August 1978).

_____, ed. *New Pathways: A Dialogue in Christian Higher Education.* Macon GA: Mercer University Press, 1980.

Fisher, Galen M., ed. *Religion in the Colleges: The Gist of the Conference on Religion in Universities, Colleges, and Preparatory Schools.* New York: Association Press, 1928.

Flannery, Austin, ed. *Vatican Council II: The Conciliar and Post Conciliar Documents.* Northport NY: Costello Publishing, 1975.

_____. *Vatican II: More Post Conciliar Documents.* Grand Rapids MI: Eerdmans Publishing, 1982.

Fletcher, John C. *The Futures of Protestant Seminaries.* Washington, D.C.: Alban Institute, 1983.

Fromm, Erich. *The Crisis of Psychoanalysis.* Greenwich CT: Fawcett Publications, 1970.

_____. *Escape from Freedom.* New York: Rinehart, 1941.

_____. *The Heart of Man—Its Genius for Good and Evil.* New York: Harper & Row, Publishers, 1964.

_____. *Man for Himself.* Greenwich CT: Fawcett Publications, 1947.

_____. *Psychoanalysis and Religion.* New Haven CT: Yale University Press, 1950.

Frye, Roland Mushat. *Perspective on Man: Literature and the Christian Tradition.* Philadelphia: Westminster Press, 1961.

Fuller, Edmund, ed. *The Christian Idea of Education*. New Haven CT: Yale University Press, 1957.

The Function of the Public Schools in Dealing with Religion. A Report on the Exploratory Study Made by the Committee on Religion and Education. Washington, D.C.: American Council on Education, 1953.

The Future Development of the Christian Education Program of the Baptist General Convention of Texas. Dallas TX: Christian Education Commission of the Baptist General Convention of Texas, 1963.

The Future of Catholic Higher Education. Proceedings of a Panel Discussion Held at the 24-25 June 1980 Meeting of Foundations and Donors Interested in Catholic Activities. Washington, D.C.: FADICA, 1980.

Gaffney, Edward McGlynn, Jr., and Philip R. Moots. *Government and Campus: Federal Regulation of Religiously Affiliated Higher Education*. Notre Dame IN: University of Notre Dame Press, 1982.

Gaffney, Edward McGlynn, Jr., and Philip C. Sorensen. *Ascending Liability in Religious and Other Nonprofit Organizations*. Mercer Studies in Law and Religion, No. 2. Macon GA: Center for Constitutional Studies and Mercer University Press, 1984.

Galbraith, John Kenneth. *The Age of Uncertainty*. Boston: Houghton Mifflin, 1977.

Gallin, Alice. "Academia and Politics: The German Experience, 1925-33." Manuscript, n.d. Revised and published as *Midwives to Nazism: University Professors in Weimar Germany, 1925-1933*. Macon GA: Mercer University Press, 1986.

Gawronski, Donald V. *History: Meaning and Method*. Glenview IL: Scott, Foresman, 1969.

Gay, Peter. *The Enlightenment: An Interpretation*. New York: Knopf, 1966.

Geier, Woodrow A., ed. *Church Colleges Today*. Nashville TN: Board of Higher Education and Ministry, United Methodist Church, 1974.

General Education in a Free Society. Report of the Harvard Committee. Cambridge: Harvard University Press, 1962.

General Education: Issues and Resources. Prepared by the Project on General Education Models. Washington, D.C.: Association of American Colleges, 1980.

Gibbon, Edward. *The Decline and Fall of the Roman Empire*. Vol.41 of *Great Books of the Western World*. Chicago: Encyclopedia Britannica, 1952.

"A Global Surge of Old Time Religion." *U.S. News and World Report*, 27 April 1981, 38-40.

Godard, James M., and J. Edward Dirks. *The Christian College and World Cultures.* Washington, D.C.: Council of Protestant Colleges and Universities, n.d.

The Good Steward. Washington, D.C.: Association of Governing Boards of Universities and Colleges, 1983.

Graham, Edward Kidder. *Education and Citizenship, and Other Papers.* New York: Knickerbocker Press, 1919.

Greene, Evarts B. *Religion and the State: The Making and Testing of an American Tradition.* New York: New York University Press, 1941.

Grisez, Germain, and Russell Shaw. *Beyond the New Morality: The Responsibilities of Freedom.* Notre Dame IN: University of Notre Dame Press, 1974.

Gross, Theodore. "How to Kill a College: The Private Papers of a Campus Dean." *Saturday Review*, 4 February 1978.

A Guide to Christian Colleges. Grand Rapids MI: Eerdmans Publishing, 1982.

Guinness, Os. *The Dust of Death.* Downers Grove IL: InterVarsity Press, 1973.

Hafen, Bruce C. "The Constitutional Status of Marriage, Kinship, and Sexual Privacy: Balancing the Individual and Social Interests." *Michigan Law Review* 81:3 (January 1983).

Harder, Frederick E. J. *A Statement Respecting Seventh-Day Adventist Philosophy of Higher Education.* Washington, D.C.: General Conference of Seventh-Day Adventists, n.d.

Harkness, Georgia. *Foundations of Christian Knowledge.* New York: Abingdon Press, 1955.

Hartt, Julian N. *Theology and the Church in the University.* Philadelphia: Westminster Press, 1969.

Hassel, David J. *City of Wisdom: A Christian Vision of the American University.* Chicago: Loyola University Press, 1983.

Heilbroner, Robert L. *An Inquiry into the Human Prospect.* New York: Norton, 1975.

Heim, Karl. *Christian Faith and Natural Science.* New York: Harper & Brothers Publishers, Harper Torchbooks, 1953.

Heisenberg, Werner. *Physics and Philosophy: The Revolution in Modern Science.* World Perspectives, vol. 19. New York: Harper & Brothers Publishers, 1958.

Hendrickson, Robert M., and Ronald Scott Mangum. *Governing Board and Administration Liability*. ERIC Higher Education Research Report No. 9. Washington, D.C.: American Association for Higher Education, 1977.

Herbst, Jurgen. *From Crisis to Crisis: American College Government, 1636-1819*. Cambridge: Harvard University Press, 1982.

Hesburgh, Theodore M. *The Humane Imperative: A Challenge for the Year 2000*. New Haven CT: Yale University Press, 1974. Reprint ed., 1976.

Higher Education and the Church: The Opportunity and Obligation of the Presbyterian Church in the United States. N.p.: General Assembly's Advisory Council on Higher Education, n.d.

Hobbes, Thomas. *Leviathan*. Part 2, "Of Commonwealth." Vol. 23 of *Great Books of the Western World*. Chicago: Encyclopedia Britannica, 1952.

Hofstadter, Richard. *Anti-Intellectualism in American Life*. New York: Knopf, 1963.

Hofstadter, Richard, and Wilson Smith, eds. *American Higher Education: A Documentary History*. 2 vols. Chicago: University of Chicago Press, 1961.

Holmes, Arthur F. *The Idea of a Christian College*. Grand Rapids MI: Eerdmans Publishing, 1975.

Holmes, Oliver Wendell, Jr. *The Common Law*. Boston: Little, Brown, 1881. 39th printing, 1946.

Holmes, Robert Merrill. *The Academic Mystery House: The Man, the Campus, and Their New Search for Meaning*. Nashville TN: Abingdon Press, 1970.

Hook, Sidney, ed. *In Defense of Academic Freedom*. New York: Bobbs-Merrill, Pegasus, 1971.

Hopper, Stanley Romaine. *Spiritual Problems in Contemporary Literature*. New York: Harper & Brothers, 1957.

Houston, William. *The Church at the University*. Columbus OH: Westminster Foundation of Ohio, 1926.

Howe, Mark DeWolfe. *The Garden and the Wilderness: Religion and Government in American Constitutional History*. Chicago: University of Chicago Press, 1965.

Human Development in the Independent College. Twenty-sixth National Institute, Council for the Advancement of Small Colleges, 14-18 June 1981. Peoria IL: Bradley University, 1981.

Hutchins, Robert Maynard. *Higher Learning in America*. New Haven: Yale University Press, 1936.

Ingraham, Mark H., with the collaboration of Francis P. King. *The Outer Fringe: Faculty Benefits Other Than Annuities and Insurance.* Madison WI: University of Wisconsin Press, 1965.

Jaspers, Karl. *Man in the Modern Age.* Garden City NY: Doubleday, Anchor, 1957.

Jeffery, David. "The Birth and Death of Stars." *National Geographic* 163:6 (June 1983).

Jencks, Christopher, and David Riesman. *The Academic Revolution.* Garden City NY: Doubleday, 1968.

John Paul II, Pope. *On Ecclesiastical Universities and Faculties.* Norms of Application of the Sacred Congregation for Catholic Education for the Correct Implementation of the Apostolic Constitution, *Sapientia Christiana.* Washington, D.C.: United States Catholic Conference Publications Office, 1979.

Johnson, Henry C., Jr. *The Public School and Moral Education.* New York: Pilgrim Press, 1980.

Jones, James W. "The Delicate Dialectic: Religion and Psychology in the Modern World." *Cross Currents* 32:2 (Summer 1982).

Kauffman, Draper L., Jr. *Teaching the Future: A Guide to Future-Oriented Education.* Palm Springs CA: ETC Publications, 1976.

Kaufmann, Walter. *The Future of the Humanities: A New Approach to Teaching Art, Religion, Philosophy, Literature, and History.* New York: Reader's Digest Press, distributed by Crowell, 1977.

Keim, Albert N. *Compulsory Education and the Amish: The Right Not to Be Modern.* Boston: Beacon Press, 1975.

Keller, Phyllis. *Getting at the Core: Curricular Reform at Harvard.* Cambridge: Harvard University Press, 1982.

Kerr, Clark. *The Uses of the University.* Cambridge: Harvard University Press, 1963. 3d ed., 1982.

Killinger, John. *The Failure of Theology in Modern Literature.* New York: Abingdon Press, 1963.

Kirk, Russell. *Decadence and Renewal in the Higher Learning.* South Bend IN: Gateway Editions, 1978.

Kliebard, Herbert M., ed. *Religion and Education in America: A Documentary History.* International Series in Foundations of Education. Scranton PA: International Textbook, 1969.

Kraybill, Donald B. *Mennonite Education: Issues, Facts, and Changes.* Scottdale PA: Herald Press, 1978.

Küng, Hans. *On Being a Christian.* Translated by Edward Quinn. Garden City NY: Doubleday, Image Books, 1984.

Lanoue, George R. *Decision for the Sixties: Public Funds for Parochial Schools?* New York: National Council of the Churches of Christ, 1963.

Laubach, John Herbert. *School Prayers: Congress, the Courts, and the Public.* Washington, D.C.: Public Affairs Press, 1969.

Lee, Rex E. *A Lawyer Looks at the Equal Rights Amendment.* Provo UT: Brigham Young University Press, 1980.

LeFevre, Perry D. *The Christian Teacher.* New York: Abingdon Press, 1958.

LeFevre, Perry, ed. *Philosophical Resources for Christian Thought.* Nashville TN: Abingdon Press, 1968.

Legal Deskbook for Adminstrators of Independent Colleges and Universities. Edited by Kent M. Weeks. Notre Dame IN: Center for Constitutional Studies, Notre Dame Law School, 1982.

Legal Deskbook for Administrators of Independent Colleges and Universities. Edited by Kent M. Weeks. Atlanta/Macon GA: Center for Constitutional Studies, Mercer University, 1983.

Lewis, C. S. *The Abolition of Man.* New York: Macmillan, 1947. Reprint ed., 1976.

Limbert, Paul M., ed. *College Teaching and Christian Values.* New York: Association Press, 1951.

Limits of Scientific Inquiry. Daedalus, Journal of the American Academy of Arts and Sciences. Vol. 107, no. 2, of the Proceedings of the American Academy of Arts and Sciences (Spring 1978).

Locke, John. *An Essay concerning Human Understanding.* Vol. 35 of *Great Books of the Western World.* Chicago: Encyclopedia Britannica, 1952.

Loen, Arnold E. *Secularization: Science without God?* Translated by Margaret Kohl. Philadelphia: Westminster Press, 1967.

Lowry, Howard. *The Mind's Adventure.* Philadelphia: Westminster Press, 1950.

Lutheran Higher Education in the 1980s: Heritage and Challenge. Papers and Proceedings of the 66th Annual Convention, Lutheran Educational Conference of North America. Edited by J. Victor Hahn. Washington, D.C.: LECNA, 1980.

Lynn, Robert W. *Protestant Strategies in Education.* New York: Association Press, 1964.

McCoy, Charles S. *The Responsible Campus: Toward a New Identity for the Church-Related College.* Nashville TN: Division of Higher Education, United Methodist Church, 1972.

McGrath, Earl J. *General Education and the Plight of Modern Man.* Indianapolis IN: Lilly Endowment, [1976].

_____. *Study of Southern Baptist Colleges and Universities, 1976-1977.* Nashville TN: Education Commission of the Southern Baptist Convention, 1977.

_____. *Values, Liberal Education, and National Destiny.* Indianapolis IN: Lilly Endowment, 1975. Reprint, Nashville TN: Education Commission of the Southern Baptist Convention, 1978.

McInnes, William C. *Jesuit Higher Education in the United States: Gaps in the Narrative.* Boston: Boston College, School of Education, 1982.

McMillan, Richard C., ed. *Education, Religion, and the Supreme Court.* Danville VA: Association of Baptist Professors of Religion, 1979.

Macquarrie, John. *God and Secularity.* New Directions in Theology Today, vol. 3. Philadelphia: Westminster Press, 1967.

_____. *Twentieth-Century Religious Thought: The Frontiers of Philosophy and Theology, 1900-1970.* London: SCM Press, 1971.

Magill, Samuel H., ed. *The Contribution of the Chruch-Related College to the Public Good.* Washington, D.C.: Association of American Colleges, 1970.

Maintaining Quality in Lutheran Higher Education. Papers and Proceedings, 1984 Lutheran Educational Conference of North America. New Orleans LA: LECNA, 1984.

Marney, Carlyle. *The Recovery of the Person: A Christian Humanism.* New York: Abingdon Press, 1963.

Marty, Martin E. *The Modern Schism: Three Paths to the Secular.* New York: Harper & Row, Publishers, 1969.

Mascall, E. L. *Christian Theology and Natural Science.* Hamden CT: Archon Books, 1956. Reprint ed., 1965.

_____. *The Secularization of Christianity.* New York: Holt, Rinehart & Winston, 1965.

May, Rollo, ed. *Existence: A New Dimension in Psychiatry and Psychology*. New York: Basic Books, 1958.

Mayer, Milton. *On Liberty: Man v. the State*. A Center Occasional Paper 3:1 (December 1969). Santa Barbara CA: Center for the Study of Democratic Institutions, 1969.

Mechling, Jay, ed. *Church, State, and Public Policy: The New Shape of the Church-State Debate*. Washington, D.C.: American Enterprise Institute for Public Policy Research, 1978.

Menninger, Karl. *Whatever Became of Sin?* New York: Hawthorn Books, 1973.

Michalson, Carl. *The Hinge of History*. New York: Scribner's Sons, 1959.

Michener, James A. *Kent State: What Happened and Why*. New York: Random House, 1971.

Michio, Nagai. *Higher Education in Japan: Its Take-off and Crash*. Translated by Jerry Dusenbury. Tokyo: University of Tokyo Press, 1971.

Miegge, Giovanni. *Religious Liberty*. New York: Association Press, 1957.

Mill, John Stuart. *Representative Government*. Vol. 43 of *Great Books of the Western World*. Chicago: Encyclopedia Britannica, 1952.

Miller, Alexander. *Faith and Learning*. New York: Association Press, 1960.

Miller, Perry. *The Life of the Mind in America*. New York: Harcourt, Brace & World, 1965.

Miller, Samuel H. *The Dilemma of Modern Belief*. New York: Harper & Row, Publishers, 1963.

The Mission of the Christian College in the Modern World. Addresses and Reports of the Third Quadrennial Convocation of Christian Colleges, 17-21 June 1962, St. Olaf's College, Northfield MN. Washington, D.C.: Council of Protestant Colleges and Universities, 1962.

Moberly, Sir Walter. *The Crisis in the University*. London: SCM Press, 1949.

Montesquieu, Charles de. *The Spirit of Laws*. Vol. 38 of *Great Books of the Western World*. Chicago: Encyclopedia Britannica, 1952.

Moots, Philip R., and Edward McGlynn Gaffney, Jr. *Church and Campus*. Notre Dame IN: University of Notre Dame Press, 1979.

_____. *Government Regulation of Religiously Affiliated Higher Education*. Notre Dame IN: Center for Constitutional Studies, 1979.

Mowry, Charles E. *The Church and the New Generation*. Nashville TN: Abingdon Press, 1969.

Mullen, Thomas. *A Middle Way: Another Look at Quaker Education; or, Will the Real Quaker Colleges Please Stand Up?* Muncie IN: Indiana Yearly Meeting, 1975.

Mumford, Lewis. *The Pentagon of Power: The Myth of the Machine*. New York: Harcourt Brace Jovanovich, 1970.

_____. *Values for Survival*. New York: Harcourt, Brace, 1946.

Mundahl, Anne, and Tom Mundahl, eds. *Vision and Revision: Old Roots and New Routes for Lutheran Higher Education*. Minneapolis: Division for College and University Services, American Lutheran Church, 1977.

Naisbitt, John. *Megatrends: Ten New Directions Transforming Our Lives*. New York: Warner Books, 1982.

Newman, John Henry. *The Scope and Nature of University Education*. 1859. Available with additional material as *The Idea of a University*. 1873. Reprint. New York: Doubleday, Image, 1959.

Newport, John P. *Christianity and Contemporary Art Forms*. Waco TX: Word Books, 1979.

Niebuhr, H. Richard. *Christ and Culture*. New York: Harper & Brothers, Publishers, 1951.

_____. *The Responsible Self*. New York: Harper & Row, Publishers, 1963.

_____. *The Social Sources of Denominationalism*. 1929. Reprint, Hamden CT: Shoe String Press, 1954.

Nisbet, Robert. *Twilight of Authority*. New York: Oxford University Press, 1975.

Oaks, Dallin H. *Trust Doctrines in Church Controversies*. Macon GA: Mercer University Press, 1984.

Oates, Whitney Jennings, and Charles Theophilus Murphy. *Greek Literature in Translation*. New York: Longmans, Green, 1944. Reprint ed., 1953.

O'Neill, J. M. *Religion and Education under the Constitution*. New York: Harper & Brothers, 1949.

Ortega y Gasset, José. *Mission of the University*. Translated by Howard Lee Nostrand. Princeton NJ: Princeton University Press, 1944.

Outler, Albert C. "Theological Foundations for Christian Higher Education." *Christian Scholar* 37 (Autumn 1954): 202-13.

Pace, C. Robert. *Education and Evangelism: A Profile of Protestant Colleges.* Carnegie Commission on Higher Education. New York: McGraw-Hill, 1972.

Packard, Vance. *The Hidden Persuaders.* New York: Pocket Books, Cardinal Edition, 1958.

Parker, Gail Thain. "While Alma Mater Burns." *Atlantic,* September 1976.

Parsonage, Robert Rue, ed. *Church-Related Higher Education: Perceptions and Perspectives.* Valley Forge PA: Judson Press, 1978.

Pascal, Blaise. *Great Shorter Works of Pascal.* Translated by Emile Cailliet and John C. Blankenagel. Philadelphia: Westminster Press, 1948.

_____. *Pensées.* Vol. 33 of *Great Books of the Western World.* Chicago: Encyclopedia Britannica, 1952.

Pattillo, Manning M., Jr., and Donald M. Mackenzie. *Church-Sponsored Higher Education in the United States: Report of the Danforth Commission.* Washington, D.C.: American Council on Education, 1966.

_____. *Eight Hundred Colleges Face the Future.* Preliminary Report of the Danforth Commission on Church Colleges and Universities. St. Louis MO: Danforth Foundation, 1965.

Pelikan, Jaroslav Jan, et al. *Religion and the University.* Frank Gerstein Lectures, published for York University. Toronto: University of Toronto Press, 1964.

Peltason, J. W., and Marcy V. Massengale. *Students and Their Institutions: A Changing Relationship.* Washington, D.C.: American Council on Education, 1978.

Planck, Max. *Where Is Science Going?* Prologue by Albert Einstein, translation and biographical note by James Murphy. New York: Norton, 1932.

Planning for Higher Education in North Carolina. Special Report 2-68 (November 1968). Raleigh NC: North Carolina Board of Higher Education, 1968.

Plato. *The Dialogues.* Translated by Benjamin Jowett. Vol. 7 of *Great Books of the Western World.* Chicago: Encyclopedia Britannica, 1952.

Pliny. *Selected Letters.* Introduction and Notes by J. H. Westcott. Boston: Allyn & Bacon, 1926.

Plotinus. *Third Ennead.* Vol. 17 of *Great Books of the Western World.* Chicago: Encyclopedia Britannica, 1952.

Pratt, Vernon. *Religion and Secularization.* London: Macmillan, 1970.

Purpel, David, and Kevin Ryan, eds. *Moral Education: It Comes with the Territory.* Berkeley CA: McCutchan Publishing, 1976.

Rauschenbusch, Walter. *The Social Principles of Jesus.* College Voluntary Study Courses, Fourth Year, Part 1. New York: Association Press, 1916. Reprint ed., 1919.

Reaffirmations. Adopted by the Association of Southern Baptist Colleges and Schools, 12 June 1976, National Colloquium on Christian Education. Nashville TN: Education Commission of the Southern Baptist Convention, [1976].

Reddick, DeWitt C. *Wholeness and Renewal in Education: A Learning Experience at Austin College.* Sherman TX: Center for Program and Institutional Renewal, Austin College, 1979.

Reich, Charles A. *The Greening of America.* Toronto: Bantam Books, 1971.

Religion and the Schools: From Prayer to Public Aid. Washington, D.C.: National School Public Relations Association, 1970.

Religion in Boston University. Report of Study Committee. Edited by William A. Overholt. Boston: Boston University, 1970.

Religion in the Church College. Authorized by the University Senate of the Methodist Church and the National Association of Methodist Schools and Colleges. Nashville TN: Board of Education, Methodist Church, 1953.

Report of the Committee of Twenty to Baptist State Convention of North Carolina. Annual Session, 10-12 November 1969, Fayetteville NC. [Raleigh NC]: [Baptist State Convention of North Carolina], 1969.

"Report of the Task Force on Higher Education." *Minutes of the 118th General Assembly of the Presbyterian Church in the United States,* pt. 1, pp. 275-76. Atlanta: Stated Clerk of the General Assembly, 1978.

"Return to Education." Transcript of the "Firing Line" program taped 27 October 1982. Host: William F. Buckley, Jr.; guest: Mortimer Adler. N.p.: Southern Educational Communications Association, 1982.

Riencourt, Amaury de. *The Coming Caesars.* New York: Coward-McCann, 1957.

Riesman, David. *Selected Essays from Individualism Reconsidered.* Garden City NY: Doubleday, Anchor Books, 1954.

Riesman, David, with Nathan Glazer and Reuel Denney. *The Lonely Crowd: A Study of the Changing American Character.* Abridged by the authors. Garden City NY: Doubleday, Anchor Books, 1950.

Ringenberg, William C. *The Christian College.* Grand Rapids MI: Eerdmans Publishing, 1984.

Robinson, John A. T. *Honest to God.* Philadelphia: Westminster Press, 1963.

_____. *The New Reformation?* Philadelphia: Westminster Press, 1965.

Rogers, Carl R. *Freedom to Learn.* Columbus OH: Merrill Publishing, 1969.

Rogers, Carl R., and Barry Stevens. *Person to Person: The Problem of Being Human.* New York: Pocket Books, 1974.

Rousseau, Jean Jacques. *The Social Contract.* Vol. 38 of *Great Books of the Western World.* Chicago: Encyclopedia Britannica, 1952.

Sagan, Carl. *The Cosmic Connection.* Garden City NY: Doubleday, Anchor Books, 1973.

Sandin, Robert T. *The Search for Excellence: The Christian College in an Age of Educational Competition.* Macon GA: Mercer University Press, 1982.

Sanford, Nevitt, ed. *College and Character.* A briefer version of *The American College.* New York: John Wiley & Sons, 1964.

Scaff, Marilee K., ed. *Perspectives on a College Church.* A Report of the Danforth Study of the College Church at Claremont, California, 1956-1959. New York: Association Press, 1961.

Schaeffer, Edith. *What Is a Family?* Old Tappan NJ: Revell Company, Power Books, 1975.

Schaeffer, Francis A. *Back to Freedom and Dignity.* Downers Grove IL: InterVarsity Press, 1971.

_____. *A Christian Manifesto.* Westchester IL: Crossway Books, 1982.

_____. *The Church at the End of the Twentieth Century.* Downers Grove IL: InterVarsity Press, 1970.

_____. *The God Who Is There.* Downers Grove IL: InterVarsity Press, 1968. Reprint ed., 1973.

_____. *How Should We Then Live? The Rise and Decline of Western Thought and Culture.* Old Tappan NJ: Revell, 1976.

Schaeffer, Francis A., and C. Everett Koop. *Whatever Happened to the Human Race?* Old Tappan NJ: Revell, 1979.

Schilpp, Paul Arthur, ed. *Albert Einstein: Philosopher Scientist.* Library of Living Philosophers, vol. 7. Evanston IL: Library of Living Philosophers, 1949.

Schuster, Jack H., ed. *Encountering the Unionized University. New Directions for Higher Education,* a quarterly sourcebook edited by J. B. Lon Hefferlin, No. 5 (Spring 1974). San Francisco: Jossey-Bass Publishers, 1974.

Schwartz, Bernard. *The Great Rights of Mankind: A History of the American Bill of Rights.* New York: Oxford University Press, 1977.

Scott, Nathan A., Jr. *Modern Literature and the Religious Frontier.* New York: Harper & Brothers, 1958.

Shenk, Wilbert R. *Mission Focus.* Scottdale PA: Herald Press, 1980.

Shrader, Wesley. *College Ruined Our Daughter: Letters to Parents concerning the Baffling World of the College Student.* New York: Harper & Row, Publishers, 1969.

Silber, John R. *The "Private" Contribution to Public Higher Education.* Boston: Boston University, 1975.

Sizer, Theodore R., ed. *Religion and Public Education.* Boston: Houghton Mifflin, 1967.

Skinner, B. F. *Beyond Freedom and Dignity.* New York: Knopf, 1971.

_____. *Walden Two.* New York: Macmillan, 1948.

Smith, Sherman M. *The Relation of the State to Religious Education in Massachusetts.* Syracuse NY: Syracuse University Book Store, 1926.

Snavely, Guy E. *The Church and the Four-Year College: An Appraisal of Their Relation.* New York: Harper & Brothers, 1955.

Social Statements of the Lutheran Church in America. (On church and state, human rights, religious liberty, etc.; adopted by the church in convention at various times since its organization in 1962.) New York: Lutheran Church in America, various dates.

Solberg, Richard W., and Merton P. Strommen. *How Church-Related Are Church-Related Colleges?* New York: Division for Mission in North America, Lutheran Church in America, 1980.

Sorokin, Pitirim A. *The Crisis of Our Age.* New York: Dutton, 1941.

Spann, J. Richard, ed. *The Christian Faith and Secularism.* New York: Abingdon-Cokesbury Press, 1948.

Spencer, Samuel R., Jr. "A Look at Five Problem Areas: What Is the Responsibility of a College?" *Presbyterian Outlook* 150 (11 November 1968): 5-6.

Sperry, Willard L., ed. *Religion and Education*. Freeport NY: Books for Libraries Press, 1945.

Spinoza, Benedict de. *Ethics*. Vol. 31 of *Great Books of the Western World*. Chicago: Encyclopedia Britannica, 1952.

The Spiritual Function of the Catholic University and Its Function as a Critic with Regard to the Ecclesial Community, the University Community, and Secular Society. Tenth General Assembly of the International Federation of Catholic Universities, Salamanca, 26 August–1 September 1973. Paris: Secretariat Permanent de la F.I.U.C., 1974.

Standards of the College Delegate Assembly of the Southern Association of Colleges and Schools. Atlanta GA: Commission on Colleges, Southern Association of Colleges and Schools, 1979.

Stark, Joan S., ed. *Promoting Consumer Protection for Students. New Directions for Higher Education,* a quarterly sourcebook edited by J. B. Lon Hefferlin, No. 13 (Spring 1976). San Francisco: Jossey-Bass Publishers, 1976.

A Statement of the Aims and Objectives of Christian Higher Education. [Raleigh NC]: Council on Christian Higher Education, Baptist State Convention of North Carolina, 1965.

Stewart, Clifford T., and Thomas R. Harvey, eds. *Strategies for Significant Survival. New Directions for Higher Education,* a quarterly sourcebook edited by J. B. Lon Hefferlin, No. 4 (Winter 1975). San Francisco: Jossey-Bass Publishers, 1975.

Stoke, Harold W. *The American College President*. New York: Harper & Row, Publishers, 1959.

Strommen, Merton P., Milo L. Brekke, Ralph C. Underwager, and Arthur L. Johnson. *A Study of Generations*. Minneapolis: Augsburg Publishing House, 1972.

Students in the 1980s. Papers and Proceedings, 1981 Lutheran Educational Conference of North America, 3-4 February 1981. Washington, D.C.: LECNA, 1981.

Summary of the 1984 Review of the South Carolina Master Plan for Higher Education. 6 December 1984. Columbia SC: South Carolina Commission of Higher Education, 1984.

Swomley, John M., Jr. *Religion, the State, and the Schools*. New York: Pegasus, 1968.

Thayer, V. T. *The Attack upon the American Secular School*. Westport CT: Greenwood Press, Publishers, 1951.

Thucydides. *History of the Peloponnesian War.* Vol. 6 of *Great Books of the Western World.* Chicago: Encyclopedia Britannica, 1952.

Toffler, Alvin. *Future Shock.* Toronto: Bantam Books, 1971.

Toynbee, Arnold J. *A Study of History.* Abridgement of vols. 1-6 by D. C. Somerwell. New York: Oxford University Press, 1947.

Tribe, Lawrence. *American Constitutional Law.* Mineola NY: Foundations, 1978.

Trueblood, Elton. *The Idea of a College.* New York: Harper & Brothers, Publishers, 1959.

_____. *The New Man for Our Time.* New York: Harper & Row, Publishers, 1970.

_____. "The Redemption of the Christian College." *Program,* September 1977, 12.

Tsanoff, Radoslav A. *The Moral Ideals of Our Civilization.* New York: Dutton, 1942. Reprint ed., 1947.

Underwood, Kenneth. *The Church, the University, and Social Policy.* The Danforth Study of Campus Ministries, 2 vols. Middletown CT: Wesleyan University Press, 1969. Reprint ed., 1970.

Vahanian, Gabriel. *The Death of God.* New York: Braziller, 1961.

Valentine, Foy. *The Cross in the Marketplace.* Waco TX: Word Books, 1966. Reprint ed., 1967.

Van Buren, Paul M. *The Secular Meaning of the Gospel.* New York: Macmillan, 1963.

Verhalen, Philip A. *Faith in a Secularized World.* New York: Paulist Press, 1976.

Vermilye, Dyckman W., ed. *Learner-Centered Reform.* Current Issues in Higher Education, 1975. San Francisco: Jossey-Bass Publishers, 1975.

_____. *Relating Work and Education.* Current Issues in Higher Education, 1977. San Francisco: Jossey-Bass Publishers, 1977.

Vesilind, Priit J., and James L. Stanfield. "Israel: Searching for the Center." *National Geographic* 168:1 (July 1985).

Vitz, Paul C. *Psychology as Religion: The Cult of Self-Worship.* Grand Rapids MI: Eerdmans Publishing, 1977.

The Wake Forest Seminar on Christianity. Wake Forest NC: Wake Forest College Press, 1938.

Walhout, Donald. *Interpreting Religion.* Englewood Cliffs NJ: Prentice-Hall, 1963.

Walker, Arthur L., Jr. "A Call to Excellence." *Southern Baptist Educator* 49:7 (April 1985): 15-16.

_____. "The Challenge of Distinctives." *Southern Baptist Educator* 49:2 (October 1984): 15-16.

_____. "Communications and the College." *Southern Baptist Educator* 49:1 (September 1984): 15-16.

_____. "Evaluating from Results." *Southern Baptist Educator* 48:6 (July–August 1984): 23-24.

_____. "Planning: Finding the Solution before the Problem." *Southern Baptist Educator* 48:1 (September–October 1983): 23-24.

_____, ed. *Directory of Southern Baptist Colleges and Schools, 1983–84.* Nashville TN: Education Commission of the Southern Baptist Convention, 1982.

Walter, Erich A., ed. *Religion and the State University.* Ann Arbor MI: University of Michigan Press, 1958. Reprint ed., 1959.

Warshaw, Thayer S. *Religion, Education, and the Supreme Court.* Nashville TN: Abingdon, 1979.

Wayne, Edward A., ed. *Developing Character: Transmitting Knowledge.* Posen IL: Thanksgiving Statement Group, 1984.

Weatherhead, Leslie Dixon. *When the Lamp Flickers.* New York: Abingdon-Cokesbury Press, 1948.

Weaver, Gary R., and James H., eds. *The University and Revolution.* Englewood Cliffs NJ: Prentice-Hall, 1969.

Webber, Robert E. *Secular Humanism.* Grand Rapids MI: Zondervan Publishing House, 1982.

Weber, Max. *The Protestant Ethic and the Spirit of Capitalism.* Translated by Talcott Persons. New York: Charles Scribner's Sons, 1958.

Weinberg, J. R. *An Examination of Logical Positivism.* International Library of Psychology, Philosophy, and Scientific Method. Paterson NJ: Littlefield, Adams, 1960.

Weinstein, Joshua. *When Religion Comes to School.* Washington, D.C.: University Press of America, 1979.

Whitehead, Alfred North. *The Aims of Education, and Other Essays.* New York: New American Library, Mentor, 1949.

_____. *Science and the Modern World.* New York: Macmillan, 1925.

Whitehead, John W. *The Second American Revolution.* Elgin IL: Cook Publishing, 1982.

_____. *The Stealing of America.* Westchester IL: Crossway Books, 1983.

Whitehouse, W. A. *Creation, Science, and Theology.* Grand Rapids MI: Eerdmans Publishing, 1981.

Whyte, William H., Jr. *The Organization Man.* Garden City NY: Doubleday, Anchor Books, 1957.

Wicke, Myron F. *The Church-Related College.* Washington, D.C.: Center for Applied Research in Education, 1964.

_____. *Handbook for Trustees.* Studies in Christian Higher Education, No. 5. Nashville TN: Board of Education, Methodist Church, 1957. Reprint, Washington, D.C.: Center for Applied Research in Education, 1962.

_____. *On Teaching in a Christian College.* Studies in Christian Higher Education, No. 6. Nashville TN: Division of Higher Education, Board of Education, Methodist Church, 1961.

Wickey, Gould, and Ruth A. Eckhart. *A National Survey of Courses in Bible and Religion in American Universities and Colleges.* Under the auspices of the Council of Church Boards of Education. Bloomington IN: Indiana Council on Religion and Higher Education, 1936.

Wiencke, Gustav K., ed. *Christian Education in a Secular Society.* Vol. 2, *Yearbooks in Christian Education.* Produced jointly by the Boards of Parish Education of the American Lutheran Church and the Lutheran Church in America. Philadelphia: Fortress Press, 1970.

Wilder, Amos N., ed. *Liberal Learning and Religion.* New York: Harper & Brothers Publishers, 1951.

Williams, George H. *The Theological Idea of the University.* The Commission on Higher Education, National Council of the Churches of Christ. Revised from "An Excursus: Church, Commonwealth, and College: The Religious Sources of the Idea of the University," article in *Harvard Divinity School.* Boston: Beacon Press, 1954.

Williamson, Peter, and Kevin Perrotta, eds. *Christianity Confronts Modernity.* Ann Arbor MI: Servant Books, 1981.

Wilson, John. *Religion in American Society: The Effective Presence.* Englewood Cliffs NJ: Prentice-Hall, 1978.

Wise, W. Max. *The Politics of the Private College: An Inquiry into the Processes of Collegiate Government.* New Haven CT: Hazen Foundation, n.d.

Wolff, Robert P., Barrington Moore, Jr., and Herbert Marcuse. *A Critique of Pure Tolerance.* Boston: Beacon Press, 1969.

Wolkomir, Richard. "Aristocratic Mice Are a Keystone of Genetic Study." *Smithsonian* 14:2 (May 1983).

Woodard, Calvin. "The Limits of Legal Realism: An Historical Perspective." *Virginia Law Review* 54 (1968).

Yoder, Lee M. "The Development of Functional Aims of Eastern Mennonite College and a Study of Their Relationship to the Organization of the Curriculum." Ph.D. dissertation, Temple University, 1979.

Young, D. Parker. *The Legal Aspects of Student Discipline in Higher Education.* Athens GA: Institute of Higher Education, 1969.